INITIATION BY THE NILE

MONA ROLFE PhD

Initiation by the Nile

The C. W. Daniel Company Limited,
1 Church Path, Saffron Walden,
Essex. CB10 1JP.

First published in Great Britain in 1976 by
Neville Spearman Limited
112 Whitfield Street, London W1P 6DP

ISBN 0 85435 093 4

Reprinted May 1986

Photoset in 11/12½pt Baskerville by
Specialised Offset Services Ltd., Liverpool
Printed by Hillman Printers (Frome) Ltd., Frome, Somerset.

CONTENTS

INTRODUCTION

We are living in a time of deep confusion and of false values. Countless thousands of people know not why they are on earth, the purpose of their lives, nor where they will be going when this life is over. In their insecurity they grasp at material goods, and as inflation catches up with their belongings, fears overcome them and they become aggressive, or neurotic.

And yet, for those who wish it, the truth is not hard to find – our origin – the meaning of our life – and the glorious experience that awaits us at the completion of the short period on earth.

During the quarter of a century in which Mona Rolfe was lecturing – her twin soul and master initiate came close to earth from the planes of light, to give an understanding of life today, by drawing a picture of the teaching given in that great temple in Atlantis, from whence masters went forth to many centres on earth, carrying the teaching and building temples in which this knowledge was given.

So we can trace the stream of light from Atlantis, brought by great masters and given by word of mouth to those who were prepared to take the tests of initiation in centres in India, Egypt, Greece, Chaldea, China, Persia, Tibet, Sumer, Arabia, and Mexico and other places. Each centre developed the teaching according to the needs of the evolving peoples, and so we find an identity of central truth in all cultures. We can trace the thread of light from Atlantis, through Egypt, culminating in the eighteenth dynasty in the wisdom and the revelation of that great soul Akhnaton. Professor J.H. Breasted, in his *History of Egypt*, called Akhnaton the first individual in history. Undoubtedly he was one of the greatest souls to come to earth. He endeavoured to build a city comparable to a 'New Jerusalem' and to give to mankind a universal teaching far beyond the grasp of the average man of his day.

We need not speak of Akhnaton in the past tense, for he is close to the earth now, guiding many souls in an endeavour to give an understanding of the meaning of a fulfilled life on earth and the glorious experience that awaits us on being released from the physical body to join the concourse of those with whom we have worked in the past and who have gone on before us. He is close to us, to help us to join hands with those on the other side of life in an endeavour to build conditions on earth in which the Christ of Aquarius can manifest.

In putting together the teachings given from the other side of life, we are dealing with happenings so remote that took place long before historical time – over half a million years ago, long before folk memory existed. Though all happenings are recorded on the akashic record and will one day be revealed – the existence of Atlantis and all that took place there is shrouded in the mists of time.

Though the difficulties of giving an exact chronological account of events are insuperable, we have been given remarkable accounts, which when put together form a coherent picture of spiritual man's gradual development through many incarnations. The events of the past have their repercussions on the present, and as the cycles of the past are replayed, similar situations occur. Those who in the past failed to complete their initiations, find the same responsibilities and burdens upon them in differing form.

The information about the past has been given us, not to satisfy our curiosity, but in order that we may have a deeper understanding of the plan of life and by the knowledge of the past, live in the present and go forward into the future. With this deeper understanding of the mistakes of the past, we can plan the education of the children of the New Age to give them strength to overcome the problems which beset them and build towards the conditions which will be necessary for the work of the Aquarian Christ.

When a master approaches the earth plane to give an understanding of timeless truths, he is partly dependent upon the power brought by the group to which he is speaking, or if

8

it is to an individual, it will depend upon the light that that soul can hold, as well as the level of his understanding.

These lectures were given over a period covering a quarter of a century – and to groups on different levels of understanding. They give a picture of conditions that gradually took shape – and slowly developed into the glory that was Egypt.

The first great temple that was built in Egypt by those who came from Atlantis was the Temple of the North, and this was situated in what would today be the outskirts of Cairo. When this was completed, the Temple of the South was built, and this was placed where the Blue Nile joins the White Nile, and where today there remains nothing but a few stones. Roughly about a hundred years later the first temple was built at Edfu, on the site on which the present much later temple stands today. These temples were primarily teaching temples and were used by those who were training for the priesthood. The doctrines and the rites held there were of a purity and glory that had come direct from the Atlantean Temples.

At the city of On, later known as Heliopolis, there grew a complex of temples. Oneferu, ninth master of Atlantis was the Healer Priest at the great central Temple of On during the period of the fourth dynasty, when the teaching given there was still of great purity, stemming from the Atlantean tradition.

The worship of Ra, the Sun God, was held there and much of the esoteric wisdom that had belonged to the Temple of Atlantis was taught.

It is a great privilege to be allowed to look behind the curtain of the past in some of the great temples of teaching and worship in Egypt and to be given a glimpse of the ceremonies that took place there.

Descriptions of various ceremonies have been given to us from a period of great purity and power in Egypt – before the darkness seeped in to destroy the light and glory. By the eighteenth dynasty, roughly fourteen hundred years before the time of Christ, evil practices had spread into many of the temples. Akhnaton, in his great desire to see the worship of the one God held in the temples, endeavoured to wipe out the dark practices and crimes which were being perpetrated in the names of many Gods.

There was in Akhnaton an immense power of devotion which he directed to the one God, whose beauty overwhelmed him and whom he saw as the power behind the sun.

At that period, men worshipped Gods with bodies like men's, and with men's passions, who were pleased when fed and flattered and who got angry for trifling offences, Akhnaton knew that over them all was the one God, who was present everywhere and was the God of all nature.

To Akhnaton the sun was the most glorious sight and he wanted all men to share his knowledge. He believed that if he could build the perfect city and a temple that would be supreme in its glory, then men would see it as an expression of truth and recognise the value and worth of the teaching.

Akhnaton was a genius, a great soul who drew his inspiration direct from God. To him the sun was the most glorious sight of all. But he did not worship the sun, he worshipped the one invisible God – whose symbol the sun was. He was hated by the priesthood when he sought to effect changes in the form of worship in the temples. He realised the necessity for the multiplicity of Gods, that each one had his place. But he knew that there was the one God above them all – and that he could communicate direct with God in the silence of his own heart. He told the priests that all men could communicate direct with God – and this they did not like; they did not wish to have the power taken out of their own hands, for they had accumulated great wealth through the power that they held.

Akhnaton's outlook was universal, and even at this early period he had a vision of the meaning of God's plan for man on earth – the oneness of all mankind; the wonder of the animal creation and the beauty of nature – the perfect balance and working out of the plan in harmony, through the various kingdoms of nature.

He believed that men could come together in understanding, without the necessity for war and that if he built the perfect city on earth to demonstrate his beliefs, the happiness and harmony that would result for his workmen as well as for his officials would spread. But he did not reckon with the hatred, avarice and intrigue of the priesthood who sought to destroy all that he built.

It was necessary for the Pharaoh to have many wives that he might have many children, and as the succession to the throne came only through the female line, his marriage to Nefertiti was one of expedience. She was not liked, in spite of her great beauty, but she supported Akhnaton in his worship of the one God. She died young from a clot of blood on the brain. This form of disability was not understood at that time, although a great deal of the working of the physical body had been discovered by the embalmers during the procedure of the preparation of the body for burial.

After the body had lain in a bath of natron for twenty-eight days, the heart and essential organs were removed and put into the canopic jars and surrounded by unguents. The operation of trepanning had already been mastered and the skilled embalmers were able to remove the entire brain through the nostrils without damaging the skull. Some of the pathologists of today are reincarnated embalmers from the past and they hold in their subconscious memory the knowledge that they acquired at that time. Surgery gained much knowledge from these practices and the study of the body after death brought understanding which was used by the doctors.

Akhnaton also died very young, for he was murdered by the priests. He was buried, as he had requested in the chamber which lies deep beneath the temple which he built at Thebes. He did not wish to be disturbed as so many others had been before him; he therefore had had a chamber prepared for himself deep beneath the temple, and this has not yet been discovered. The tomb which has been excavated and is believed to have been his, was that of a substitute who took his place.

So much was destroyed by the priests that there is very little concrete evidence on which the archaeologist can build his theories. Only two of Akhnaton's beautiful poems remain to tell us of the depth and beauty of his teaching, his understanding of the oneness of all creation, and that the sun

11

shines alike on all men whatever the colour of their skin. Yet even in our day, men are killing each other for the mere difference in doctrinal points and very few have reached the supreme vision that Akhnaton held and put before men.

The temple at Tell-el-Amarna was a great achievement in architecture, and its furnishings and decoration were of a superlative beauty into which Akhnaton poured all the fineness of his soul. Although the surface temple was destroyed, deep beneath the sands of Egypt there remains a glorious edifice, which may one day be uncovered by the winds of Egypt – even as it was covered by storms and wind after the destruction of the city.

In considering the vastness of the conception held by Akhnaton long before the majority of men had reached a state of understanding at which they could accept his vision, we realise that the sacred knowledge had been brought from Atlantis and had been given to the initiates in the temples by those great masters known as the 'Bati', each of whom reigned for a hundred years before returning to the spheres of light.

The worship of Ra, the Sun God, had been held in the temples where the true esoteric teaching was given from the earliest times in Egypt. The tradition was carried on in the Temple of Teaching at On, and that great soul, the twin soul of Oneferu – Oneferua incarnated again in the eighteenth dynasty in the person of Queen Tiy or Queen Thitos. She it was who gave the early teaching of the one God to her son who was then known as Amenhotep the fourth, and who later took the name of Akhnaton. He was also guided by Menaton who had held the position of highpriest healer at On in an earlier incarnation and whose divine name was Oneferu. In the eighteenth dynasty Menaton was at first highpriest in the temple at Thebes and later at Tell-el-Amarna. And so we see the direct link with the teaching from the Temple of Light in Atlantis brought down through the successive dynasties.

It has puzzled the archaeologist that Akhnaton should have held so exalted a vision at that early period, and that he should have had such unique understanding. Sir Flinders Petrie, in his *History of Egypt*, having quoted from the shorter version of Akhnaton's hymn, says of it, "It would tax anyone in our days to recount better than this the power and action of the rays of the sun. And no conception that can be compared with this for scientific accuracy was reached for at least three thousand years after it."

We know from tablets in existence that for some time after Akhnaton's accession he acted as a minor under the tutelage of Queen Tiy. His title – 'Son of Ra' emphasises his close connection with the old Sun cult of On, in which his religion had its roots.

Nefer-Kheperura – 'Beautiful essence of the Sun', and Ua-en-ra, 'Only one of the Sun' are to be found throughout his reign in all inscriptions concerning him. He was also known as 'Favourite of the Two Goddesses', and 'Beloved of Amon-Ra'. And his name in later days was accompanied by the inscription 'Living in Truth'.

He was dominated by the idea of the oneness of an immaterial God – at a time when no other man held so exalted a concept.

No other man had seen the sun as the supreme source and embodiment of all that appeared to him to be worth adoring: beauty, power, heavenly majesty, as well as that great quality, kindness.

The distinctive symbol of the new religion was the sun's disc with rays ending in hands. Akhnaton had no quarrel with any of the Gods, not even Amon. His God was above them all.

An inscription in the tomb of Ramose at Thebes tells us that the King had already grasped the truth which he had received direct from God and which he knew intuitively.

On the tomb it says – 'It was known in my heart opened to my face – I understood.', and Ramose answers, 'Thy monuments shall endure like the Heavens, for thy duration is that of Aton therein'.

Akhnaton wanted to start a new tradition, more rational, more scientific, more beautiful, more truly religious, on the basis of his extraordinary individual insight, to raise the state religion of the future to his own level – to make himself consciously divine man – the special head of the nation – which he would teach how to transcend nationhood.

During his reign, art attained a level of naturalness and

13

truth to life that it had never reached before. The magnificence of the great reception hall was one of the wonders of the world. His new city, besides being of a beauty and glory beyond our conception, was also a religious centre and an industrial town.

The Pharaoh had built a model settlement. He built a model of what he would have desired the world to become under the beneficent teaching of truth.

He recognised the sun as the source of heat and light – rain and all cosmic occurrences. The sun, apart from being the condition and cause of life in general, he saw as the ultimate regulator of each individual life. 'He setteth everyone in his place', and the differentiate of races and of their characteristics. The idea of a God of all lands and not just a national God was entirely new.

Historians and archaeologists on finding similarities between the great cultures of the world seek to trace the connection between them as the result of influences reaching each other through travellers and through contacts at some point.

Because the existence of Atlantis was prehistoric, they leave out of account this all important connecting link, the source of all knowledge.

For millions of years the esoteric teaching has been held in secret, behind closed doors for the initiate alone, and for those who spent their lives in the temple, and the secret doctrine was passed down through word of mouth.

But in the Aquarian Age much of the wisdom held in secret teachings will be prepared and given out to all who are ready to touch the esoteric doctrine.

The young scientists and physicists of today are building a foundation of factual knowledge which when shown to be a part of the esoteric wisdom will form a solid structure by which it will be possible to demonstrate to mankind the purpose and pattern of his being and the meaning of his life today and will give a vision of the future beyond his present conception.

Betty Shephard.

CHAPTER ONE

The Etheric Temple between the Temple of High Heaven and the Temple on the Heights

There came a moment in God's Plan for man when He first put out His desire that man should no longer worship Him in the etheric glory of light of His Presence, but that he should be prepared to carry that light, power and colour to other planets, other places, than the place of the Hierarchy.

Because the work of the Father-Mother God is always made and prepared and commanded in the form of a cycle or circle our Father-Mother decreed that man should go forth and then return. He knew that it would be aeons of time before man could return to the same condition that He had left, but He knew that certain forms of creation were to come into being through which those who knew and understood the nature of God would carry light, and prepare members of other creations for their work in service, and that one day they, too, might return on the cycle of evolution and become pure light.

The Father-Mother God decreed that man should undergo many changes. He created the ball of fire which is known as the original and first Earth, the ball of fire which whirled through space and gradually became cooler and cooler as it slowed down to its immense circular progress.

Upon that planet there came the first light, the casting off of a vibration of light and colour and sound, which put itself out in such a way that it was caught by the cooling planet and held there. It grew and became life in very primitive early stages, until the great Temple created by the Father-Mother

God had prepared, through its teaching, those who were ready to go out and people that planet with the light of the Presence of God.

The Hierarchy surrounding the Father-Mother God joined together morning and evening in the Great Praise, and in the beginning the Father-Mother God created for Himself Son-Daughters in His own image, some of whom should descend to the earth plane, others of whom should remain beside him.

Gradually, below the great Hierarchical Temple there was built and prepared an etheric Temple, the exact counterpart of the Hierarchical Temple, but of a slightly denser ether, and into that Temple were guided and directed students of the great Hierarchical Temple, students who had learned and studied under the Hierarchy and knew all sound, vibration and colour.

Thus there came into being the great Temple in the ether, between the Temple on the Heights and the Temple of High Heaven; an exact copy of the Temple of High Heaven, it produced, for the service of God, the same great praise in the morning and evening and carried out the same routine, if we can use such a word for such a great achievement, in the etheric planes, planes which would correspond in our minds today with those planes above the Garden of Remembrance.

When that cycle of evolution was complete – you read in your *Book of Genesis* – 'the Lord God planted a garden', and here you have the first touch with what you call the soil'; a garden so vast, so enormous that the mind of man today cannot possibly visualise it; a garden in which from time to time there walked the high priests, the healers and the teachers from the great etheric Temple, having the power to descend to a slightly denser ether and to leave behind them in the garden the great vibration they carried of light and sound and colour.

Out of that merging of light and sound and colour there came together stones, precious stones, formed from these vibrations and filled with the light and the power of the Father-Mother God. These stones were shaped in such a way that each one had its own place in the foundation of the Temple on the Heights, for the great garden was prepared

16

by the Father-Mother God for man, not for Himself, that man might have a place wherein he could find God within the Temple of Nature, to which he would return at the end of his day, weary and sad and disappointed, to gain power from the trees which the Father-Mother God had blessed and from the soil.

It is that picture especially that we need to hold in our minds for the future, because it is that point to which we are returning. We are finding the confusion of the material life intolerable, and all over this country there are many, in other countries also, who are unable to bear the strain and the stress on their sensitive etheric bodies of the great cities and have withdrawn from the cities into the silent places, the lonely places, and are endeavouring to build within the soil a garden where the Lord God may find rest and peace.

Unfortunately, many of these young Aquarians have gone out before they were ready, their youthful training has not helped them to form any foundation, and therefore they have missed that point on the cycle of the past, which touches the creation of the precious stones. They will find, sooner or later, that they will not be able to hold on, because in undertaking this life in the hills and the valleys from the ways of men, they have built without the material foundation of the precious stone which holds the light, the sound and the colour of the Father-Mother God.

It is the point we have reached at the moment and for a while we must learn to walk through the confusion of men, the confusion of our city traffic, of the people hurrying to and fro, choosing where we can, to walk in the quiet by-ways of the city rather than to join that hurrying crowd, remaining poised and strong, strong in the knowledge that once upon a time we watched these very stones being prepared for the foundations of the Great Temple. We saw their glory, the glory of light and colour, we heard the sound which they emitted, sweeter than the song of any bird in the material world, and we touched that life in that great Temple on the Heights, with a knowledge and a wisdom which is still veiled for us today.

If we were able to touch the wisdom of the past and to bring it through in its completeness it would be our undoing, for we

17

would become creatures unable to face the storms and confusion of material life, and our mission lies in the life of the material world.

We have come to learn to produce the light of God from within ourselves, like tiny candle flames in the darkness, to shed it round us, so that man may feel satisfied and happy in our presence. It does not matter if they think we are peculiar people. It matters not at all, but we shall find far fewer who consider us peculiar than the number of those who will come to us again and again that they may obtain that something from us which we hold from the light.

So that in reality our feet are still standing on the foundation stones of the temple, those radiant glorious stones which could not be broken, and no such tool as a hammer or chisel could be used upon them. They were precious stones; the only thing that could carve them away or cut them in pieces or divide them up was the power given by the Father-Mother God from the temple in the etheric plane of light, power which came direct from the Father-Mother God to those who ministered in the Temple of the Hierarchical Host, but power which must be filtered through the channels of the members of the Hierarchical Host, that they might pour that power out upon those who dwelt in the coat of skin upon the Atlantean heights.

What was this coat of skin? It was man's first body. It was of ether, not unlike what we call ectoplasm today. It was formed from the denser ethers which surrounded the spirit of man sent out in service, but it contained also the power and the light of God and it held the vibration of the stones which concerned the individual priest, or the individual student, so that the power which came through the priest poured out through his finger-tips, in such a way, so that in its communication to the stones it shaped the stones to the desired shape of the temple. It moulded the soft transparent pieces, that they should form a coloured, chequered floor in the centre of the great temple.

The vibration of groups of angels' wings, you call them 'wings' but they are not really wings, they are light and power and sound, were gathered together at the four corners of the great carpet of coloured stone and hung like tassels at the corners. Had you looked at those tassels they would have dazzled you with their light. They carried the one colour, the one ray, the one sound of the highpriest. They only became alive and alight when the highpriest himself ministered in the temple, and as he held his hands up, as all members of the priesthood whatever the denomination or the country do today, the colour which he brought into the temple from the Father-Mother God Himself, poured out from his finger-tips, radiating among the people who were assembled in the temple itself.

The power, light and the sound ceased only when the highpriest held up his two fingers and that was the moment when the children assembled in the temple and bowed the head and the knee to receive the blessing of the highpriest.

Over the coat of skin there was no garment. The coat of skin was radiant; its foundation of white ether, with the colours of all collected sound pouring through it, so that it would look opalescent, or radiant according to the amount of light that was taken from the highpriest by the assembled congregation.

There were moments when the highpriest would turn his back to the congregation in order that he might renew his power after it had been absorbed by the people assembled in the temple. But they all wore the coat of skin; they all belonged to the temple, they had all been given their own special duty and service by the Father-Mother God at the moment of their departure in such a way that they remembered it. Although, when they crossed the threshold of the temple they left behind them the rays which had joined them with the foundation stones of the temple, they nevertheless, carried out with them as a cloak, the glory of the light of the temple itself given to each one of them by the assembled multitude, guided and directed by the highpriest.

CHAPTER TWO

Life in Atlantis

If we go back in thought to the moment of the planting of the garden we can get an idea of what really took place in those times which seem so far off and yet are so closely linked with the souls of many today.

The great and glorious temple with its twelve subsidiary temples attached, had already been built for some time upon the Tableland of Atlantis, and that temple was the Temple to the Most High God, in which all who served, whether as priests or lesser priests, servant, warden, or steward, and it is in that order that we must take these degrees, and later as gardener, wore the coat-of-skin.

The coat-of-skin would be invisible to the physical eye of most people today. It was of a clarity unimaginable and it was pure with light and encompassed by the great rays which were poured forth all day long by the Spiritual Hierarchy which surrounded the Father-Mother God.

The highpriest ordered a garden of flowers and herbs to be prepared upon the slopes of the great mountain on two sides only, where it led down into the valley, so that round two sides of the Temple was a garden which contained all the flowers and herbs, and the other two sides were a green sward. entirely lifeless except for the life of the grass, and that side was known as the Garden of God because it should not be planted until the Lord God commanded His special children of the Breath to plant that garden.

On both sides of the hill where the gardens of flowers and herbs were planted, there were pathways leading down into the valley, and at this time there were as yet no living souls in the valley. In the temple, when the time came for the highpriest's work to be finished he was called to ascend to the Father-Mother God and his place was taken by the priest who had stood on his right hand, and the Bard, or third priest, who had functioned from the left, came and took the place of the first assistant priest, and his place was taken by another who was the Master of musical sound, for the third priest ministering in the temple must always be a Master of musical sound even to this day.

Each time a highpriest ascended to the Father there came into being two lesser Stewards, who were born of the Breath fully adult, living souls within the coat-of-skin, and each one would bring his offering to the temple, an offering of service in some form or another, either an offering of music, or needlework, or building, or designing, or preparing the colours which were used in such profusion in the great Temple of Healing. But healing was not the healing you know today. Healing was the merging of soul to soul in perfect harmony. Healing was harmony, but it was apart from the musical sound which was used as pure sound only in the temple, that pure sound which was later captured by that great shell known as a conch, but which has in reality an esoteric meaning. It was a shell prepared to capture sound. That is why the temples of the East hold ever in their ministrations a conch shell, which is used for the production of pure sound.

When the moment came, the Father-Mother God saw that it was good and He commanded a garden to be planted, and that garden was to receive the ministration of all who at that particular moment served in the temple, and it took many, many years in your time to plant. For the seeds of that Garden were not as the seeds of the flowers on the other side of the hill; they were the seeds of mighty trees which could continue to live, year after year, after year, so that their greatest age could hardly be numbered in time.

Each one who served the temple, and there were already many hundreds of workers in the coat-of-skin, went forth at

21

the bidding of the highpriest and he planted a seed which eventually grew into his own tree, his contribution to the Temple of Light, his grateful thanksgiving to the Father-Mother God who created him, his token and symbol from the beginning of time of his own affected self, his soul enfolded in the Spirit of the Father-Mother God.

So for awhile the green sward was still green, and then all over it, down the two sides of the hill, came these tiny shoots which grew together, some quickly, some slowly, until the great Garden of God, which was nothing less than a forest, came into being. But it took a very long time.

In the meantime there came into the valley, by the Will of God, beings who wore rough garments but did not serve the temple. These garments were of a texture which later became the physical body of earth. They were not created Children of the Breath; they were created by a word of power, a word of power which brought into being men and women in the likeness of the temple beings, who were holy and blessed in the sight of God, and they dwelt among the growth of the valley, which was coarse, thick and ugly, not unlike your great jungles in Malay today.

These beings brought their children into being as tiny infants, and when the servants of the temple were guided down the hill to visit the children of the valley, they were amazed and astonished when they saw these tiny images of the parents, brought into being in an unusual way to them, who were accustomed to seeing their contemporaries come into being of the ethers of light, which became set and almost solid before their eyes to form the coat-of-skin.

From time to time, the priests made pilgrimages to the valley. One pilgrimage which was made regularly was the pilgrimage in search of the Golden Rose, but the other pilgrimage was in a sense a missionary one. For those who dwelt in the temple felt that these children of the valley had very little, if any, sense of duty, or understanding of sound, and therefore, they wished to carry that understanding and teaching to them, and they would take with them their healers whose task it was to bring the beings of the valley into harmony with each other, so that the notes they came to utter should be harmonious and of the same tone and strength.

All who served in the temple, from the highpriest down to the humblest person, and he would be the gardener, spoke no word at all. Speech did not exist, only sound, and each, from the humblest to the highest was called upon as part of his temple training to study sound in all its purity, in all its strength, in all its beauty, to utter his own note upon the ether so that it sounded like a great bell. It is from this sound that have come to you today your peal of bells. It is the sounding of the notes upon the ethers of light which originally produced those sounds. The movement of sound in the ether produced colour and, therefore, all who served the temple, from the humblest to the highest, must understand colour, must recognise it by its sound and by its texture and must be able to distinguish colour used in a certain ceremony, from the colour used in another ceremony, and although all colours later became reduced to three primary colours, there were no such things as primary colours in the great Temple of Light.

No one could pass to the world of spirit from the temple, until he had fulfilled his service, or his work to the Temple. He may come in as a young soul, a child of the Breath nevertheless, and have to serve and work his way to the position of highpriest, but he could not pass into the world of spirit until he had fulfilled his complete cycle of service and learned and studied all there was to study of the service and the priesthood.

When he had completed his service his being became light; just as you draw light to yourself, towards your own light within and send that light of yours from within to without to shine, it was something you learned in that temple, so there would come a moment when your whole being would become light and you would just disappear from the sight of your fellows. You would appear to float; you would be taken in light.

Everyone who served the temple was born under a symbol, those symbols given by the Father-Mother God at the creation of his soul, and when that soul was considered by those in the etheric worlds who fulfilled that service, fit and well enough to return to God, having completed his service, that symbol

23

would be shown in light above his head for a short period of time, before he was gathered to the Hierarchy.

Things were very different in the valley. To begin with there were very few people in the valley. They did not understand light or sound or colour. They had no communication with each other except by touch, and their children had no speech. They did not come into the world with a cry, nor did they ever learn to speak. Their parents spoke not. But from time to time, there would come into incarnation in the valley one who was sooner or later called to serve the temple, and when that soul arrived, the priest would be informed intuitively in the temple and he would send a steward of the temple down into the valley to find the whereabouts of the child expected, and this steward carried a staff and on the staff would be imprinted the symbol which heralded the child's birth, thus linking the child with some steward, or some servant of the temple who bore the same symbol on his brow.

That child and the growth of that child would be watched very carefully by those who served the temple. There would most probably come a moment when he was ready to be educated in the temple and he would approach the temple with the knowledge that he had gained in the valley. When that moment came, the only way he could reach the temple was by levitation and, therefore, the warden or steward who was responsible for his education in the temple, would send out the necessary light to bring him in the ether and, of course, still in the body of the valley, into the temple itself.

The incarnations in the valley increased with a much greater speed than in the temple and, therefore, there came a moment when it was inadvisable for the steward to go himself in search of the child who was his responsibility. It was found that when he did so he was surrounded by these strange beings, who made these peculiar guttural sounds, who had no culture, because they had no knowledge of the value of sound and light and colour, and they would draw from the steward the temple light which he carried, so that he would become heavy in the etheric body for lack of light, and frequently could not return to the temple himself but had to be sent for and carried himself by the power of the messenger, back into the temple, where he would lie for a long time as if dead, upon a couch of stone in the Temple of Healing, the Temple of Healing which was the Temple of Harmony, the blending of sound and colour and light.

So it became necessary for an etheric messenger to be sent to the child of the valley, to warn him that the time was approaching when he would be expected to come to the temple and prove himself fit for service. This messenger, moving swiftly among the people of the valley, would not excite the curiosity of the people, because he would wear the garb of a gardener and they were already used to the gardeners who attended the flowers and the herbs on the hillside in their view. They could not approach the hill, because there was an invisible etheric barrier, but all the same, they could see them, even today as you would see a vision, moving about among the flower beds, in coarse rough garments.

Such a one would withdraw the child he sought into a quiet place apart from the haunts of men, and there together, using the creative word, which is ever one of the greatest gifts of God, they would draw blades of green living growth and small saplings and weave a bench, and upon that bench the child would be left seated, when the messenger returned to the Temple. He would rejoin his family and his friends; but the mere fact that he had made contact with the messenger, alienated him and people would be a little afraid of him in the valley, and he himself would feel a desire to make contact with that wonderful radiance and glory which he had touched when he moved beside the messenger – the light of the Sun, and he would therefore depart from his friends in the valley and find the sheltered spot where the plaited seat remained.

Thus the soul who was ready to take that next great step, was set apart from his fellows, and a link was made from the temple to him so that he received the power for the building of an etheric cape, or canopy around him.

This was the first time that that method of building an etheric canopy had been used, and although we are familiar with it today, it had never existed until the moment when the child of the valley had reached such a point in his progress, in the body of flesh, that he was able to be admitted to the temple by the power of levitation of the physical body.

The bench played a very great part in all things connected with the temple and it also played a large part in early Egyptian history. It was upon this bench that the neophyte reposed until the coming of the priest from the temple.

When the priest approached him he brought with him a great power of light, but he could not use that light until the light within the neophyte had also shined. Therefore the soul must be ready for the coming of the priest and the priest would be best content if, on approaching that place apart, he found the one he had come to fetch sitting with humility, his hands folded before him and his eyes closed, in readiness for the great ascent. For he would know that in that quietness, the light of the spirit from within would shine forth and in that light, that greater light which was necessary for the levitation would shine and grow and become strong enough to fulfil the way.

The priest who came from the Temple wore the coat-of-skin, therefore he would be invisible to the people of the valley. He would appear, perhaps, to some as a passing light, even as you see the sunlight through the leaves of a tree taking a shape upon the ground. His feet would not touch the ground; he would descend through the ether, his feet never far from the ground, but at the same time the body in a posture which marked him as one not of the earth and the earthly body.

When he approached the one he had come to fetch, he would stand before him, that the radiance from the solar plexus of the priest should fill the solar plexus of the student, that the power of light which surrounded the priest should be merged in that of the student, and thus they would both be gathered under that etheric canopy.

The etheric canopy would appear to the eyes of the priest as of many lights and it would also be full of sound, for the sound of the temple is as of many bells at. eventide, a harmony of bells and bell-like notes which it is not possible to describe in words.

They would sit awhile together, the student and the priest, and because of the similarity of the symbols which they bore there would be an affinity between them, a sympathy, a looking at one another, not with the eyes of a stranger, but with the eyes of a friend.

The light would glow and radiate, yet the people of the valley approached not, nor were they conscious of the light, for they were of gross matter, humble clay, creatures in the body of flesh, seeking to fulfil a strange animal-like life, with the exception of one or two who sought something higher.

When all was ready the priest would sound the single bell-like note of the sound 'OM', and the note would vibrate upon the ether and the ether would be light with sound, and the group of priests and servants in the temple who were seated waiting in the inner sanctuary for the arrival of the priest and the student, would be silent but also very conscious of their coming.

As the light note of threefold sound died away, the priest would take the hand of the student and the student would grasp the hands of the priest and both would be lifted from the ground and borne away from the valley, upward to the Temple on the Heights.

So came into the life of the people of the valley that first taste of the knowledge of death. They would be conscious for awhile that one of their number was not quite like them, that the brutish animal nature which they possessed was not shared with this one particular soul, a soul that sought the solitary places, who would listen to the song of the birds and watch the glow of the sunrise and the sunset and tread the grasses of the valley with care that he crushed them not, and handle the children of the valley with love and understanding, serving always with humility and yet giving them to feel that he was greater than those he served.

They would watch him and sometimes they would move away from him; at other times they would seek more than usual to serve him in their turn, greeting him as one who was greater than they. Subconsciously they would know that there would come a time when he would move away from them and so they said that he had been called, when others asked where he was. They did not know where he was. If they were conscious of the bench of plaited grass and twigs in the quiet

27

place in the forest they said nothing about it. They knew that he would withdraw into a silent place and in that silent place he would remain for a while apart from them. They knew that during that aloneness he would have no need for physical sustenance, that he was just waiting, and they knew that he could not be called to wait there unless he had heard and been conscious of the call. They would not ask within themselves what the call was, but when he did not return they would say he had gone away, and later, when speech came to the children of the valley they would call it 'dead', they said that he was 'dead', the one who had departed from them. Where his house was they would place a stick to remind themselves of him, and later that stick became a crook, and from the crook was made the ankh, where the loop of the crook was held down close. So the first symbol of the life of man was erected in the valley.

They would know that he would not return, and perhaps from time to time, one who would be the next to be called would be conscious of movement in the ether round him as he walked. Perhaps he would raise his head and shade his eyes and see the student and the priest moving through the ether even as the hands of a swimmer displaces the water, as he swims, and that would take shape, or form in their eyes. Later, they would try and depict that form by drawing with a stick upon the ground and the shape became a pair of wings. Sometimes they would add the features of the one they had loved who had loved them, to the wings, and that looked strange without a body, so in the soil with their pointed stick they would draw the face and draw the body and draw the wings, and here you have the second symbol of the men of the valley in the 'Ka', the soul which journeyed through the ether away from the shadows of the hillside into the light.

And as the people in the valley increased, it became more difficult for the soul to manifest its light in those who should be called, and such a one would go deeper and deeper into the forest and plait himself a bench of reeds and boughs, and because he had moved far away from his friends, he would need to spend many 'days' in that part of the forest, and he would need protection, so he built his bench a little higher, and when he was drowsy, he would sit beneath it, and because the sun was hot, he would pluck the leaves of the trees and weave them in with the branches of the bench to make a shade for himself, and there he would wait for the priest. And so here you have the first 'tomb'.

When the people of the valley went out, as they did when they became more numerous, to see what had become of their fellow, they would find the bench, which would be empty, but sometimes they would find a cloak or an outer garment which their son had worn and that would be left beneath the bench, and because they reverenced him and loved him, and because they had no explanation at all for his disappearance, they would shut this garment in carefully, by weaving sides to the bench after the manner that the son had woven the seat of the bench and they would weave leaves in with the twigs and the boughs, so that none could see within. So you have the first tomb, and that tomb was called in the Atlantean language 'Mus tub ai'; it became later part of the Arabic tongue and in Arabic there are many words which are similar to the words spoken by the Atlantean people. Such a word would be formed of sounds and you can imagine people without speech, uttering these three syllables upon the ether – 'Mus tub ai'. These are the words of primitive people, which have been held for all time in cultured tongue, and that word means 'the bench', which later became the 'tomb'. For if we study the origin of the tomb of the Pharaoh and the Pyramids we continually come across the Arabic word 'mastaba'.

So the bench became the holding place for the garment of the beloved, the earthly garment which was worn by the people of the valley, woven roughly by the hands from grass, not unlike the rough tunic later adopted in many countries for the slaves and serfs, but nevertheless a nature garment for the covering of the physical body, to prevent the sun from scorching the skin and the wind from cooling it so that it felt the cold. That was the great difference between the coat-of-skin and the physical body; the physical body was conscious of heat and cold, the etheric body, or coat-of-skin was conscious only of light.

29

CHAPTER THREE

The 'Lookers' in the Temple

We have reached a period of time when man was called to adopt the physical body of flesh and to compress that etheric body of light into such a compass that it could be held within the physical body, and just as the servants and the wardens and the stewards of the temple were the first to be clothed in the body of flesh, so were the priests the last to be clothed, and the last of all the highpriest. Masters dwelling behind the veils during certain periods of time brought back the expression of the will of God for His servants.

The mechanism of the body was not at all an easy thing to handle, or understand. These beings who had been accustomed to functioning in etheric bodies of light and later in the coat-of-skin, as perfect twin-souls, were now separated and each told to go their own way. You will realise how difficult it was, because the female portion of the twin-soul holds the intuition and the male portion is the portion that acts, that works with action on the intuition of the female portion, and whereas the two were functioning in one as one, here they were divided and although for many generations of men the twin-souls were together, yet the separation in the actual physical body had now to be accepted.

There was no division of thought and very little division of action. The twin-souls were similar in features and build, but nevertheless the one had the gift of intuition and the other had the gift of action, therefore there was a dividing line when they were separated which they found very difficult to understand and to accept.

The functions of the male in the world of men then became entirely different from the function of the female, and that needed consideration and understanding also. So that there was a long period of time when the Temple on the Tableland was in a state of instability, of being unable to settle to its ordinary work, and because the vibrations were troubled, the Masters, the highpriest healers, were no longer able to return to the place of light as they should have done, and little by little it became understood that the highpriests must themselves function also in the physical body, they also must later on be separated, so that the male and the female inhabited two bodies in place of one, and that therefore, a different method must be used to obtain the guidance direct from God, which was necessary for the conduct of the temple and the conduct of the children of the earth.

Here we touch for the first time that group of women who were known as 'Lookers' and who were set aside for the purpose of seership. They could not be chosen except from workers in the Temple. Their training was difficult because they had advanced beyond the first stage of understanding, the gift of looking, therefore, it was realised that children must be accepted into the temple and dedicated to the work of the Father-Mother God in such a way that they went not outside the temple, but made the temple their vocation and their life.

Therefore children were admitted, and because they were admitted there came also to the temple women to care for the children and other women to teach them their first lessons in temple service, so that a very large temple retinue grew beyond the confines of the major temples, the central temple of spiritual worship, with its twelve surrounding temples. Therefore, there grew a greater building, in which were housed the children of the Temple, who were called to the service of Lookers.

It was found that the boys had of course no gift of vision. Therefore, it was always the female souls that were chosen and they were trained from their earliest days in the discipline of the temple, to walk softly, to wear the white temple garment

31

with grace and beauty, to be able to set aside a portion of each day even when they were very young, in prayer and meditation in the temple.

With these inner exercises, there went many outdoor exercises, to keep the physical body cleansed and purified in the air and the sunshine.

Water played a large part in the exercises of these children, for great swimming baths were in the gardens of the temple where they spent many hours of their day.

They learned to walk through the rhythmical music of the temple pipes, the wooden pipes of the temple. They learned themselves, to prepare the pipes of reeds and hollow stalks, that the notes therein might be sweet with music.

Above all, they learned the indoor rhythmic movement of the body, which is wrongly named the dance, for it was not a dance. It was a rhythmic movement of the body which brought into play all the organs of the body in turn and exercised these girls, so that they were supple and strong in youth.

About the age of ten they would be taken for the first time to the Master Initiate, the highpriest of the temple, for their acceptance as Lookers. During their period of training in the temple they became very much aware of the world from which they had come and of the worlds through which they had passed. Therefore, they would be conscious of the world of spirit through the light which surrounded the highpriest and in answering his questions, they would accept that power of light which he gave and brought with him and be able to use it in answer to his questions.

After they left his presence, each was given a horizontal mirror, not the kind of mirror you hold today, but a precious stone, not unlike the diamond, planed and smoothed, and backed with some dark material so that the light was held within the surface.

For many months these children would be trained to look within these mirrors, to see there the colour and the light and the symbols of the spirit world.

Their lesson in looking would take a large part of each day and it would always be undertaken early in the morning after the night session of sleep, and fasting. They would partake only of water before they undertook this lesson.

As they went forward in their training, their vision would deepen and in addition to the vibration and colour of the world immediately around them, they would see mirrored in their glass the colours of the higher world of spirit.

They would journey awhile in their looking in the Garden of Remembrance. They would watch in the mirror the arrival of souls on the other side of life after the change called death, and they would be called upon to notice the difference between those who went over from the temple, or the temple garden service and those who went over from the valley. The colour and the light and the vibration would be totally different.

From time to time they would attend the Master Initiate and he would speak with them of their looking and also of their movement and exercises in the temple rhythms. For the temple rhythms expressed the psalms and the songs of the temple ritual. Every movement had its meaning. Every movement to the highpriest who watched these children in movement, portrayed for him a symbol of one or other of the planes beyond the normal consciousness of man.

As yet these children had touched nothing of darkness. They never left the temple precincts. They spent their happy times in the gardens and by the great river, and in the movement which kept their physical bodies in rhythm and perfection, they found their recreation.

They were in the charge of a mistress who was known as the Mistress of the Novices, and many of those women who held that position in Atlantis returned in life down the ages to rule and govern the great convents of the Christian Church. Therefore, they brought with them the memory of the temple ritual and the exactness of their demands showed from whence they had learned the beginnings of their lessons.

There were three stages or tests to be passed by the Lookers before they were granted the second mirror, for in the holding of the second mirror a certain danger lay. With the one mirror it was possible to link direct with the world of spirit, but with the two mirrors there was mirrored in the upright mirror the events and happenings in the material world, and therefore, the student must be very strong in light and power, to be able to accept at the hands of the Master Initiate, the second mirror. These mirrors were not joined. They were rectangular, and they were held by the lookers, one horizontal and one upright at the back, and again a period of training in vision gave the Looker an opportunity of reading the past and the future.

A method was undertaken through which novices were trained to read the mirrors, under the guidance of a priest of light. The test for this reading was severe. It lasted a long time and frequently the lookers became very weary. They were taken away from their studies from time to time, usually once every period of three moons on the waning moon, to return upon the new moon waxing. Therefore their work was done in that short period of time which lies between the waning of the last quarter and the new moon. And that is the time today when all those who have still the gift of vision are able to see into the ethers of light and give a description of their vision and their finding.

The mirrors today represent a danger, which only the highly-trained medium can understand and avoid. Therefore it is not for the student to attempt the looking.

Sometimes you will find as you sit before your own mirror, that you see the ethers around your face changing and the light rising and falling and the colour enfolding your features. Do not think that you have returned to your place in the temple as a looker. That is natural; if you have any gift of clairvoyance, you will be able to see that in the mirror yourself, but do not attempt to make a practice of it, and do not at any time attempt to use the two mirrors, the one horizontal and the one upright, for it was through those two mirrors that the great danger came into the Temple of Light.

The mirrors were fixed only in certain pillars of the temple, and each novice knew the pillar by which she must stand and knew where could be found the tiny knob, or button which must be pressed to reveal the mirrors.

Even if a peeping Tom were to watch where the novice found the knob that opened the cavity and returned when the Temple was quiet himself to do it, the knob would be invisible

34

to all but the novice who understood it.

There was no question of trance at this period. There was no question of retreating during the hours of sleep and bringing back memories which were taken down on the tablets. Only from time to time and at certain periods the Master Initiate of the temple would call for the service of the Lookers and the student and the bard as you know them, but in reality they were the minstrels of the temple, who would inscribe upon the tablets the words and the findings of the lookers themselves.

CHAPTER FOUR

The Temple of Healing in Atlantis

There were many beautiful temples in the past which were used for the healing of the souls and the bodies of men.

In Atlantis there was a temple set on a hillside: perhaps you would call it a tableland, for it was like the flattened top of a hill set upon the side of a great mountain. It looked over the valley on two sides, and it faced another temple on a similar plateau on the opposite side of the valley.

Many men and women have come back on a cycle which touches directly a very important life, or position in that life in Atlantis in the past, and they spend their time trying to recapture that Atlantean glory instead of realising that because they made mistakes they must redeem that glory, and learn with humility as little children, how to use the power in service to humanity.

This temple was circular in shape. It was known quite simply as the Temple of Healing. The only light which entered it, that is, the central portion of it, entered at the top, where the walls joined the vast dome, and the dome was adjustable, so that sunlight, either pure or filtered, could be poured through the roof, or could be prevented from pouring its power into the interior of the building.

The entrance was rectangular. It was built of intensely white, glistening stone, stone which looked as if it were filled with mica and colour, and the heavy crossbeam of stone which spanned the doorway had sculptured upon it a white swan with its noble head upraised, moving gracefully outward.

There were groups of pillars composed of the precious white stone, which was bendable but could not be broken, which were moulded to form a perfect circular upright, and the steps were rectangular, in the same white glistening stone as the building itself. There were no gates, or walls to guard its gardens, for pleasances lay around the great Temple, and the gardens were filled with blossoms; great beds of marigolds in their season, tulips, sunflowers, and many of the small, sweetly-perfumed roses. All gave of their glory for the healing of the people.

Within the entrance was a large hallway to right and left. Round the central circle were to be found two wide passages leading to the three special temples, which were to be found at the far end of the central building. These temples were also circular. They were not entered, nor was there any entrance, from the main temple, but the entrances were through doorways heavily curtained, opening upon these passages, which stretched to the right and the left of the main temple.

The central circular temple was the small special temple, where the healers studied and were trained, and on the right of that temple was the Temple of Teaching; on the left the Temple of Research – not research in the sense that you use it today in connection with material things, but research into all which concerned healing of body and soul.

All the teaching was undertaken in the Temple of Teaching. All the training of the healers, where they were used as instruments and were not required to make use of their mind or brain, was undertaken in the Temple of Healing, and all the research was undertaken in the third Temple. Students who came to the Temple of Healing were obliged to become proficient in one of these arts, and were allocated and placed, either in the Temple of Teaching, in the Temple of Healing, or the Temple of Research. They were not allowed to follow the three courses at once; they had to prove their proficiency in their first choice before they were permitted to take a second, in one of the other temples.

The central Temple of Healing was built over a lake, and you will find its counterpart very often today in the swimming baths which can be covered by a wooden floor, but in this case the floor was of amethyst, precious stone, warm to the touch of naked feet, and radiant with light and power.

At the entrance to the central temple were the robing rooms for the priest healers, the students and the novices, all built of this glistening white stone, and, although austere, very beautiful, in harmony of colour and design, in the various hangings and woven materials which were used for their beauty.

Between the robing rooms, which were not unlike the cubicles in one of your great swimming baths, ran a passage-way, and again other sets of cubicles which were used for the cleansing and purification of the bodies of the patients. Healing in those days was not a matter of a few moments as it is today; a patient from the valley would be required to come many times to the temple for the purification of his physical body. The hair, which grew long in the children of the valley, was cut to the nape of the neck during their period of healing, and following the baths in plain spring water, they passed through baths of perfumed warm water, before they were given the white linen garment, in which they presented themselves before their healer.

In the first of the smaller chambers of healing, they must pass the purification of the etheric body, and there, the healers, with the power of clairvoyance developed and strengthened by their service in the temple, would watch for any dark places, or lack of light in the chakra and in the etheric body as a whole. The patient would only be permitted to go forward into the next healing chamber when the priest healer in charge of this particular room could report an etheric body cleansed and full of light.

In the next chamber most of the patients would spend very much longer than in the first one, for here the weariness of the mind must be released, and as the mind relaxed and the body, in harmony, relaxed, the patient would talk to his teacher, telling him of the anxieties that troubled him and the weariness of soul which oppressed him. This is what you call psycho-analysis today, and it is a long process; it is also a very risky process, for if you go to a psychologist for psycho-

38

analysis he must observe you for quite a long time before he dare begin to probe within your mind, lest, in chasing out one devil tormenting you on the mental plane, he should leave the door open for seven devils to enter. Therefore, the work undertaken in the mental room was of a very specialised nature. Only the greater and more experienced priests handled these patients, and many hours of the day were given to complete relaxation and pleasant conversation, and the partaking of fruits for the cleansing of the physical body, the pleasant juice of citrus fruits and the spring water, which was so valued as part of the healing work of the temple.

When the patient had passed the necessary tests, he would move out of this second temple and into the temple for the healing of the physical body, but not until all the ugly side of his personality – hatred, jealousy, the bitterness of envy, and selfishness – had been completely cast away; for so long as any grain of envy, or hatred, or jealousy rests in the mind of a patient, the body cannot entirely be whole and cleansed.

In the great central temple there were three sessions daily, for the healing of the sick. In a gallery which ran round the great building below the level of the windows, were men and women students who were trained in music and singing, and in this gallery they were conducted, during all healing operations in the temple below, in the singing of rhythmic chants and spiritual songs, which gave of their glory to God.

Twelve healers under one leader worked upon twelve patients. The beds were erected on white marble, built like rectangular boxes, the top made of this same precious stone which could be bent but not broken or cut, and each bed was composed of the stone of one colour, representing one ray.

When the patient left the last healing room, he was given a six-pointed star in the colour of the bed which he must occupy. This star he gave to the warden in charge of the patients of the temple, and it was strapped upon his forehead by the warden, so that the moment he entered the great healing chamber, the healer who belonged to that particular healing table would beckon his patient. As soon as the patient lay upon the healing table, the radiations of his aura would project, as an emanation round the head and the body, thus lighting up the whole of the corner of the room in which he lay, and opening for himself the power to absorb the ethers from the soil and the surrounding light ethers.

If it so happened that any patient lying on the bed did not radiate these ethers, then the healers beside that particular bed would stand motionless, until the whole of the eleven others had been treated by their healers, and the patient would be obliged to return to the preparation on the mental plane, to learn a further period of relaxation. But this rarely happened; the patients were prepared and completely relaxed when they reached the great healing chamber.

There were four healers to each bed; the Priest Initiate on the right, the second priest on the left, the third and fourth priests on the right and left at the foot. The Priest Initiate directed the healing and the two at the foot poured power through the feet from the palms of their hands. Each healer wore a garment of the colour of his own ray, and a cloak over the shoulders of the same colour. During the healing operation this cloak, taken by the corners, would be turned back, fastening at the hem by a jewelled clasp. This little operation was performed by those who were beginning their healing training and were known as novices.

The ablutions of the healers were performed according to the direction of each Priest Initiate in charge, the hands being laved with running water at small vessels, placed in the wall behind each healing bed. When the healing was completed, a period of roughly half-an-hour to an hour of relaxation was demanded of the patients, and at the end of that period the healers would retire and the wardens take charge of their own individual patients, conducting them back to the robing room, where they were given a meal of honey in the comb, crushed corn and milk, and sent away to their own homes.

The healing continued ceaselessly during the daylight hours from dawn until dusk, but was never performed after sundown. That is why so many who are working on high vibrations of healing today find it extraordinarily difficult to undertake the healing of a patient after sundown. This does not refer to absent healing.

40

CHAPTER FIVE

The Atlantean Influence in Chaldea

Atlantis suffered destruction on three separate occasions, occasions which were separated by long periods of time and which were marked by quite different natural phenomena, phenomena which were used in the destruction of the continent.

On the first two occasions only a portion was destroyed, but on the third occasion our Father-Mother God saw fit to destroy all things that He had made in their most complete fulfilment. On each occasion messengers went forth at the bidding of our Father-Mother God to carry His power, His teaching and His understanding, to the four corners of the earth, and the occasion which we are touching, because it is nearer to our time and further from the planes of light and, therefore, will be more easily apprehended by those who tread the path of earth, is the third occasion.

This third time, thirty-six Master-Initiates went to the East, and these Master-Initiates were chosen, not from the great circular temple on the tableland, but from one of those twelve great temples on the other hills, which was entirely rectangular, with a strange pinnacle at the top, in which was held the inner Sanctuary of Light.

We are speaking of a civilisation of ancient times infinitely greater than the civilisation of today. We are touching in these Master-Initiates men who knew God, not men who were acquainted with Him as with a name, but men who knew

41

Him, who revered Him, who worshipped Him, who knew His power and His strength and His holiness, who knew the meaning of spiritual law and knew what it meant to encourage men to consider the law of God first and foremost in their lives.

There was no conflict among men in the going forth of these great ones; the conflict arose after they had departed, and it was a conflict of the elements.

These thirty-six Master-Initiates went away by the command of our Father-Mother God to the East, twenty-four of whom went to China and to those great tracts of land which lie on either side of that country, and twelve were directed by the finger of God to the Euphrates valley, and it was there they found a simple, uncultured people living and communicating with each other by gestures and strange sounds, people of very little progress, who knew not God, and who sought only the cultivation of the soil and to live from day to day, even as the majority of men today.

These Masters did not journey alone; they took with them those who could assist in the government of the Temple, and they took with them also their students and their novices, chosen ones only, who were suitable physically for the great journey, and suitable spiritually for the work which they had to undertake.

We will touch very briefly the conditions of the Euphrates valley; of the lush vegetation due to the heavy flooding of the great river and its tributaries; of the beautiful natural gardens which were to be found extending for many miles on both banks; of the trees which were so much like the trees in their own country of Atlantis, that they felt, as they descended into the valley they had indeed found home. For there were glorious fruit trees filled with ripe and perfect fruit, where pomegranate trees and orange trees and great vines growing stationary upon their own stems, lifted up to the sunlight that their fruit might ripen, asking no artificial assistance to stand upright in their place.

These Master-Initiates commanded their workmen to go forward and to seek among the children of this great valley men who knew timber and how to prepare it, men who knew how to prepare all that was needed in the building of a temple. They explained by signs to these children of the valley that they had come, not to supplant them, or drive them out, but to build in their midst a glorious temple where God could dwell, and they took as their example, because it was eventide only when it was cool enough to have speech with these people, the glorious disc of the Moon, with its rays around in silver.

These people of the valley, standing outside their simple huts and dwelling places at eventide, looked up to the sky and pointing out the moon to each other explained to those who knew not what they meant, that these wise men who had come from so far away, had come to build a house for this wonderful ball of light and that when the house was built the ball of light would rest within it, so that its power could strengthen and warm all men.

Because they knew the work which they were performing they came together readily with the men who had come from Atlantis, and they girded themselves and carried out all that was necessary to prepare a portion of the great valley for the mighty Temple. But the workmen from Atlantis realised that these simple people had built their dwelling places upon high platforms and therefore there must be some reason why they should not build them on the ground, and it was decided that they should wait awhile and prepare all that they had to prepare, but not to choose the place for their temple until they had seen a portion of that period of time which you call a year, finished.

And lo and behold: when the moment came for the leaves to fall on the ground, from the trees, and when the fruit was gathered and enjoyed by all, the mighty river rose within its banks, and the water poured on both sides. Then the healers from Atlantis came together and said, 'Lo! this is a mighty miracle, for here we shall have much water for our healing work. We must harness this water, so that at our command it will come to us and enable us to perform our healing among these people who are crippled with sores and twisted limbs.

So they realised that they could not build their temple in the valley as it was and they realised, too, that they themselves could not be happy in the valley, for they were accustomed to

43

great hills from which they looked over wide spaces of country, wide valleys and great mountains, so that they, when they began to build their temple, must build it upon a high foundation. So with care they prepared this foundation, and many hundreds of men came running, and women and children also offered their services, in this great work.

They prepared bricks of mud, square blocks, which they set to dry in the sun and they prepared bitumen which was used for the sealing together of the blocks, and they built great drainage courses which should draw away the water at flood time from the foundations, and they drove tree trunks into the soil, until they had built a great rectangle on which they could erect their temple. And the foundation was already five times the height of a man.

When they placed the second portion of the building upon the first one, they built on the outside aprons of mud, cemented together with bitumen, in such a way that when the rains fell the water would flow from the building itself.

Night and day they worked upon their temple, and it was a long, long time before it was completed, and within that temple there was no single straight line, no chamber which was entirely rectangular with the whole, for these men who built that chamber also come into the picture when we speak of ancient Greece. The model of the temple, had you been able to cut it down the middle and look at the inside, was the model of the Parthenon in Greece and of other buildings of similar proportions.

Finally, the temple was complete and perfect in all its details, and wise men came from Eastern countries who had heard by word of mouth from those Master-Initiates who dwelt among them, that already in the valley of the great river were men who were building a mighty temple, and brought their offerings of wood, spice and gums, of silks and precious hangings, and of fillets which have part in the inner sanctuary of every temple, to the chief Master-Initiate.

Within that temple was completed an inner sanctuary, but this sanctuary was set in a little conical house on the very top of the temple, and there dwelt, and was cared for, their Oracle; she, who from time to time was called upon to deliver the word of God to the highpriests, but was never permitted to approach the lesser priests, or those of the valley.

These priests, who had come from Atlantis, knew much of the value of sound, of melody and colour, especially, too, they excelled in the making of instruments of strings, and wondrous harps brought they, inlaid with fine gold leaf, whose strings when touched did give forth the melodies of heaven. Lyres, and strange flat instruments from which your present cello is copied, were also made, and much harmonious melody sounded within the temple precincts.

When the temple was complete the highpriest Initiate called all who were ready to enter, to leave their shoes upon the threshold and to walk with great humility bare-footed within the whole central portion of the temple. And here, within this great temple, which came to be known as the High House of Chaldea, was practised for the first time wonderful mystic rites, which are known to you today in a very much debased and lesser fashion, as the mysteries of Masonry.

Here did the highpriest Initiate, placing himself and his lesser priests upon the chequered carpet with its four tassels, stand and call to the Moon Goddess that she should bless this work which had been begun, and here within this great and mighty temple there rose such a glory of etheric sound that the voices of the men, those who dwelt in physical bodies, were completely soundless against it, and yet they, too, did try and join in the harmony, realising that they were touching an ascension of sound, even as today you memorise in your hearts the Ascension of the Master Jesus. So was the Ascension of Sound celebrated in the Temple of the Moon.

Time went on, and other Initiates came to replace the first Initiates. The second Initiates, finding the temple not high enough, did build another on top of it. When the third band of Master-Initiates came, they built another temple – an exact copy of the other, still higher upon the top of the first two temples, thinking that thus they could draw closer to the Moon.

The Moon Goddess blessed their work; she brought fertility to the soil, she made their fruit trees to blossom and to bear rich harvest; she brought the waters of the river to their door,

45

but not to swamp their dwellings, for the moon controls the water and all that deals with the living waters of our Father-Mother God.

Within the temple, at the time of the third coming of the Master-Initiates, the esoteric rites increased in secrecy, and those who were not ready, or perfect in their training and understanding were shut out, and as they became more secret they became more exclusive, and gradually there grew up in the country called Chaldea a mighty band of powerful men who wore in their secret sessions the great white conical hat. What is the meaning of that conical hat? It is like a dunce's cap which you wear today sometimes in fun, but it is much higher and much harder for it is made of a translucent white stone which can be bent to the shape of the cap but not broken, and from the apex of the cap hangs a small badge or charm, denoting the age of the wearer, whether he belongs to the second, or first, or third degree, or whether he belongs to the last degree of all.

Those who met to make use of the power which was given to them were a fine body of men, intellectual and strong and full of courage, and the power they used was the power of white magic, known as the power of the Moon Goddess, which was borrowed from our Father-Mother God.

Then there arose a race within the land who knew not God, and these usurped the power of the temple and desired to make things happen more quickly, and instead of using the white magic power of God to bring things to pass, they allowed Satanaku, the evil one, to function. Listening to his desire to hasten progression, they stooped to the power of darkness, and from the moment that the darkness entered that great and mighty temple, there was bewilderment, and the great white hats became cloudy and dull, and the badges of their rank and position fell from them, and they stood as little men who aped the great Father-Mother God, trying to draw from the Moon power which would help them to usurp the power of God. And they forgot God; they forgot that in the Inner Sanctuary of Light they could find God and hear His Voice; they forgot that the glory of God ever overshadowed them and that they alone made the barrier of darkness, and,

46

trying to strengthen their power, they placed a black band round the brow where the white conical hats touched them.

Those mediums who are given the power of seeing the aura of those who come to them for guidance know when they see the conical hat, whether it belongs to the great and original Temple of the Moon, serving God in all its glory in the Inner Sanctuary of Light, or whether it belongs to the great darkness which entered with Satanaku, and prepared the way in Babylon for the temple which is known as the Tower of Babel.

The size and the height of this temple is beyond description but, as in all things which came from Atlantis, a day will come when it will be unearthed, and the excavations which have been made so far are as nothing to the beauty which shall be unveiled when the power of darkness is removed and the light exposed.

CHAPTER SIX

The Atlantean Influence in Babylon

The times that we are dealing with represent many, many thousands of years ago. The buildings which were discovered by those who excavated Chaldea and ancient Babylon represented buildings which had been erected by men twenty-three centuries before the birth of Christ, but these are modern times compared with the times which we shall touch upon.

For these are matters which are timeless. Atlantis is part of the great scheme of our life, even though it is so remote, but it will come into the Aquarian Age most forcibly, and therefore we must know what to look for, by what signs, by what materials, by what flowers and vegetation we can know those portions of the world which still have Atlantean influence working through them.

In Atlantis there were many temples. A temple in Atlantis was not only set aside for religious worship. Every cultural art, and what you would call 'profession' today, was housed in one of these great buildings. There was no religion in the more material type of temples, because God was with men and, therefore, all men knew His Presence and all men gave Him the authority and the obedience to which He was entitled as their Father-Mother God. It was only when men grew away from God and did not realise that He was their Father, that these more material temples became gradually buildings empty of power, empty of that great over-shadowing love of the Father-Mother God, and thus in many cases, empty of that guiding hand which men need so much today.

You have two examples of these great temples in which the hand of God still moves, the Voice of God still commands obedience, and one of these temples is the Church, and the other is the Law. If we could place your great universities back into Atlantis, they would be called Temples of Learning, and if we could place your great House of Architecture back in Atlantis, it would be called a Temple of Architectural Design, and the palace of the ruler would be the Temple of Administration, and so on right through.

In many of the universities only a portion can be penetrated by the world of spirit. The majority of your universities today are so much given over to hard scientific material facts that God is forgotten, and therefore the university as a whole cannot always be considered a temple of learning, because a temple is a house of God. Those of you who visit the great university cities, and are sensitive to the power which surrounds those ancient buildings, should be able to tell whether they should be called temples or not by the vibrations you touch there and by the atmosphere which encircles them, but in that special legal sanctuary where matters of spiritual law are dealt with by those who guide the fortunes of men, we can safely say it is a temple, even if, from time to time, there comes to trespass upon that sacred ground one or other who is given over to the works of darkness; and that one will find his place precarious, so precarious that if he is conscious at all of the Ancient Wisdom at times the ground beneath his feet will veritably tremble and fill him with fear. But whether those who guide the fortunes of men are able to hold these temples sacred, they are still places for God in the midst of the material world of men.

Before coming to the great Temple of Babylon which came later to be known as the Tower of Babel, we will touch a group of twelve Initiates from the twenty-four who went further north than the Euphrates valley when they left the Atlantean tableland, and who settled in that great country which you now call Northern China.

It is important to those who are students of these matters,

because just as we are living the incarnational cycles of Atlantis and Egypt through today, so must we touch the incarnational cycles of Northern China when we return to fulfil our work in the Aquarian Age, for the new age of man, for which man is preparing himself today, will find its centre in a portion of the globe which will be known as Northern China. It will touch the most beautiful portion of that great country which you know as Siberia, portions of which, even today in spring and early summer are glorious with blossom and as beautiful as the Garden of Eden.

When these Atlantean Masters went forth to China, they founded quite different temples from those who descended to the Euphrates valley. Their temples were pyramidal in shape and were surmounted on the great hills which stood around the valley, for the temples were never built in the valley. They erected places of seclusion where they could dwell in meditation and train their students and their novices, for the rites of the Temple service.

Only one of these great temples exist today and that is in the form of a pyramid somewhat larger than the pyramids of Egypt, and built of a strange glazed brick, the secret of which is not known today. It stands in a desert so lonely, so windswept that the foot of man has never touched it. This was the great Temple of the Gathering, the temple to which all who worshipped in the other temples of that portion of the globe, journeyed at certain stated seasons for initiation into the Inner Mysteries, and for the understanding and the receiving of the power of the spirit. All around as far as the eye could see, nestling on the hillsides were these strange monasteries, or places of seclusion, where men ate and slept and worked and prayed, as any modern monk does.

The evil which came to that portion of the globe, for it was not free from evil practices, was of a more subtle and devastating nature than the evil which touched the temples of the Euphrates valley, for it tried to tear down with its knowledge the planes of spirit. It was an over-development and an over-manifestation of the psychic powers of man, an over-balancing so insidious, so dangerous, that there dwelt within these monasteries many men who, from long fasting

50

and long meditation, should have been able to join hands with the angels, but who remained little grey lumps of flesh and blood, self-destroyed by the psychic force which they drew around them.

That is one of the chief reasons why those who are incarnate today should clear their Atlantean and Egyptian incarnational cycles before touching this particular and important cycle in China, which deals with some hundred years following the third exodus from Atlantis, and why it is so dangerous for them to hasten their development.

As you can imagine, when those first Initiates went out from Atlantis to the Euphrates valley they were homesick and alone: instead of their great and beautiful mountains on which they had erected temples of great beauty, they were faced with flat, wet valleys, in which any foundations which they laid would be destroyed during the seasons of the floods; this is why they built their temples in tiers well above the ground, so that they appeared like huge erections which no-one could have taken for a temple.

The Master-Initiate in charge of the initiates realised that he must prepare one special temple, for when he left Atlantis he had been commanded by his Father-Mother God to bring the children under his charge two or three times in every period of every cycle of the seasons, to a special gathering, in order that they might receive the power of the Holy Spirit – that power which in the Bible is called 'the Holy Ghost'; and as a modern example you have the Holy Ghost descending 'like a dove' to the Master Jesus, that much-loved child of God. So was it essential that all those who served the great temples should be able to come together, apart from the busy ways of men, and leave their planting and their sowing, their bricks and their building, and their daily tasks, and gather close to our Father-Mother God, for the gift of the Spirit.

Why could not that spirit power be poured out upon men just anyhow in the streets and the market place and where they fulfilled their daily task? Because this power of the Spirit was the greatest and most perfect gift that God could give those who had already served Him with strength and love and obedience; it was therefore necessary to call these aside from

51

time to time, that they might dwell in that great etheric bliss. Here they could find that etheric bliss and at a height apart from the busy ways of men and in that silence worship the glory of God, and through that worship receive the gift of the Holy Spirit – that gift which made everything clear and plain. The souls who were ready and were accepted for the giving of the Spirit were those whose eyes would be opened and whose tongues could be loosed to declare the glory of God. For their understanding, their learning, was above the learning of those who were not the created Son-daughters of their Father-Mother God; the gift of the Spirit, the renewal of that Holy Spirit had been poured out upon these great Atlantean Masters when they left their glorious temples and their heights of peace and their great gardens and their wonderful trees, to descend into the plain to bring the message of Godhead to the children of earth, and to try and show the light to Satanaku, the rebel, that he might eventually lead the children to the light instead of the darkness.

For the building of this temple the great Master-Initiate, known as the First Master, under the guidance of God, did command and supervise the building of a great and mighty temple on a portion of land which later came to be known as Babylon, and it was at Babylon in the erection of that first wonderful and mighty temple, that all these thirty-six Masters from far and near gathered to receive the gift of the Holy Spirit, at a moment which followed the moon which you know today as the Wesak moon, and at the moment following the Spring planting.

Here they dwelt within the glorious temple chambers for many days, fasting and partaking only of water and fruit juice and of wild honey, in their desire to clear and purify their bodies for the reception of the Holy Spirit, and when that great morning dawned they gathered together at the very pinnacle of this great temple, and holding out their arms to the power of God, they called with one voice upon Him to bless them and their work for Him, by pouring out upon them and renewing within them, the gift of the Holy Spirit.

Not only did our Father-Mother God Himself descend from the planes of light to enfold these great Masters with the glory

52

of Himself, but hundreds of thousands of the Heavenly host, moving as if on invisible ladders, up and down the sides, and in and out and around the great temple, sang praise to Him.

Here you have the legend of the great and mighty gift of Tongues, for thus these men were gathered from the corners of the earth, though they were worshipping in a valley far removed from their own homes, they had dwelt long with God; they had forgotten the language that He spoke, but at that moment all understood and all shared in the glory of His Presence and the joys of His commands and the understanding of His words of praise.

In commemoration of this great out-pouring of the Spirit, the Master-Initiate commanded that a small temple be built not far from the entrance of the great temple or tower, and that this temple should be called the Temple of the Tablets. Here, on wonderful blue stones were inscribed the records of this great and mighty happening, and in the central courtyard of this Temple of the Tablets was placed a circular, glistening, marble basin. It was placed upon a pedestal, and it drew its source of water from the Water of Life, this water being poured forth through an enormous water-lily, the type of lily which preceded the lotus blossom in Egypt, a lily which had grown only within the Inner Sanctuary of the Temple on the Heights, and had not even survived in the tableland – a great white glistening glow of light, pure as crystal, gushed forth the water from the centre of this blossom, and all surrounded with the blue stones, the tablets on which were inscribed the names of those who had partaken of the gift of Tongues.

Father handed this memory down to son, son handed it down to grandson, and so on, down through the ages, so that when a crisis eventually occurred in Babylon and the people wished to rise against the King who ruled them, they prayed that the gift of Tongues might once again be vouchsafed to them, and not only was the gift of Tongues granted to the people of Babylon in their hour of crisis, but the Temple of the Tablets was filled with flame, not the flame of fire which consumes and burns, but the flame of the Spirit which purifies and strengthens the heart of man and gives him power to go on.

53

CHAPTER SEVEN

The Atlantean Influence in Greece

Before we consider the influence of the Atlantean Initiates on Ancient Greece, we need to realise the meaning of our mission in this day of time.

The limitation of the memory of civilised man is considerable compared with some of those whom you would describe as savages, and a group in particular of these so-called savages who dwell upon the Gold Coast of Africa, who have a memory which is quite incomparable. They can remember occasions and incidents in many lives; they can remember when they are old men, incidents of their babyhood, and, in addition, they can see very clearly their path in the future.

What is this quality which, in the untutored savage, is found with the greatest ease as part of his life, and yet in Western civilisations, not only is the memory of previous lives extremely dim, but even present memory is dim also?

You cannot go very far in the understanding of the ancient mysteries unless, as you touch those mysteries, you can reawaken your memory. Only when you reawaken your memory can you see the plan adjusted in all its perfection, and can you realise and understand the working out of spiritual law which is the law of God, and only then can you take your place with any satisfaction to yourself, or to those who guide you on the incarnational cycle of life.

Why is this? Because there are certain people and groups of people incarnate in the western world today, who, like the dark-skinned men on the Gold Coast, have been granted the special privilege of coming to earth with that memory slightly, or strongly developed.

This memory does not awaken as with a clap of thunder as one long distinct history; it is awakened by every little incident which goes to the making up of your life. As you achieve victory over some fault or failing, as you readjust some karmic debt of the past, there you see clearly where and when that debt was incurred, and you see also why you are back in this particular period of time to awaken the memory.

These incarnational cycles must be completed before you can go forward to the next cycle. Sometimes there is something which is blocking your progress, because you have not awakened the memory which has led to that block and which you must clear before you can go forward.

We are not back in incarnation today as individuals to represent individual personalities in the past. We are here to take our place on an incarnational cycle which must be completed and achieved before our next cycle is attempted, and a certain number of these cycles must be completed before the dawn of the Aquarian Age. We cannot allow darkness from the individual, or the group, to spoil the beauty of the Age of Aquarius. It must be cleared, and it must be cleared with knowledge and manifestation of the spirit in addition to material and physical suffering, material and physical loss, or giving up, and material and physical, as well as spiritual achievement.

Atlantean influence in Greece is of very great importance. You speak of a temple as a place of religious worship, but in the worlds of light a temple is any great and beautiful building raised to the glory of God in which art and music and learning can all be infused by spiritual power to find their achievement.

We have a Temple of Light and a Temple of Learning, a Temple of Records, and a Temple of Administration, a Temple of Healing, a Temple of Religious Worship, and so on, and each temple has its Holy of Holies, its innermost Sanctuary, where the mysteries of God are learned and understood, from the angle of the work of that particular temple.

So far, the Master-Initiates whom we have considered went out to the East, to China, to Chaldea and the Euphrates valley, being a fertile and glorious place for them, where they raised great temples to the glory of God for religious worship – temples which had each its own sanctuary, its own dwelling place of the Most High, where men came who would be learned in spiritual law and the mysteries of God, where they knew they could meet the created children of the Breath and draw from them power and love and light and colour.

A group of Master-Initiates went to Greece and divided into three portions. One portion, the smallest portion, comprising only four Initiates in all, came to that little country – insignificant sometimes in your eyes – which you know as Ireland, and the remaining thirty-two divided into two groups, one descending into Northern Greece, and the other descending into Southern Greece to that portion of the country now known as Corinth and Arcadia. They brought a very wonderful culture with them. They were not highpriests of religious worship; they were highpriests of another culture. The temples that they represented were temples of science and learning, of music and of art, and of the first group that left Atlantis their art consisted almost entirely of sculpture, and everything which could create out of stone and marble and mineral, the beauty of God, and demonstrate spiritual law.

It is doubtful if throughout the land of Greece there will ever be excavated temples which were used for religious worship like the temples of Egypt. These temples were for creative work, for the worship of God through art and music and science, which means knowledge.

The memory of their own Atlantean temples was very strong with these men, and because of the great beauty of the country in which they settled and the great culture which they established – a culture which was kept glorious even down almost to our own times, many of the ancient gifts of the Atlantean priests of culture are still to be found among the country people in the very north of Greece and in the south. Here you will find in many cases that the language has been debased by the admixture of other tongues, but there are many finely built, strong, simple hearted young men and

56

women of today, still to be found in those great mountains and valleys who can remind you entirely of Atlantean culture, who do the manual work which they are undertaking today, with all the grace and beauty of a cultured race. In the South particularly the ancient memory needs very little refining, for if you could find a patch of Atlantean soil and bring it with you and place it in the hand of a chosen peasant of southern Greece, so quickly would the psychometric touch unfold, that he would picture for you the Atlantean tableland and the Heights.

These first Atlanteans who journeyed forth to the great temples of Greece established such glorious happiness in this lovely fertile country that they prepared a wonderful foundation for the two groups who later followed them and helped to build the glorious Temples of Learning and Art and Beauty, of which we can see the remains.

Greece should touch you very closely, for many of you who have sons and daughters between the ages of twenty and thirty-five are most probably conscious of certain characteristics in their make-up which make them stand apart. Many of the young people of that age are reincarnated students from these great temples of culture. You have applied to them your modern educational system, and in many cases it has failed because they took no interest in examination successes.

These are children of a great generation, restless and uneasy because they can find no dwelling place in this untidy world. If you would take them to visit the ancient monuments of Greece, if you would help them to an understanding of Pythagoras and the work of Aesculapius, how they would open and unfold. Your educational system is altering somewhat and you are making room for some of the younger children who show their creative ability. You class them as 'B' children and yet these are greater far in soul and in place in the plan of life than any of those who take the material world in their stride with examination successes.

If the children who are now between twenty and thirty-five years of age had studied law, how wonderfully they would have unfolded and developed their consciousness, for many of them belonged to the great Temples of Law in Greece, law which means not the doing down of your neighbour, but justice administered with authority and balance – the logical application of the law of God working through the life of man.

These young reincarnated Greeks take to law and the study of it as a fish takes to water, because they have within themselves the power to awaken and understand spiritual law, and therefore, if we give them a material basis for those studies there will no longer be restlessness and lack of employment and constant changing from one place to another. They will adapt themselves to life, and with that learning of the law and the spiritual strength which it will bring them, every door of employment will open to them.

This applies also to sculpture and music, but in both these cultures the outward and visible sign of materialism is apt to rivet the mind of the student to the exclusion of the memory of the past.

The children of tomorrow are the children who will respond far more readily to the music and the colour and the form of the past. Many of these are incarnated through Irish parentage because of that small powerful and wonderful group that settled in that green Ireland, a group which, for its knowledge of the colour and sound of the heavenly places, was quite incredible in its glory, and which has left within the hearts of its people the power to hear and to see the world of spirit, and thus awaken ancient memories and strange and beautiful sounds, vibrations in which the discarnate soul can speak to his loved ones.

CHAPTER EIGHT

The Temple of Light and the Temple of Darkness in Atlantis

Atlantis was partially destroyed once, slightly more on the second occasion and completely destroyed the third time. It is the third time that we now touch and although some of the pictures are not so beautiful, we realise how closely, ugly as they are, they resemble the world of today. And we realise how we have become involved in these cycles which must perforce be replayed before Atlantis can rise again and glorify God in all the beauty of the cleansed and purified place of Peace.

During the first and second Atlantean epochs the Temple was not entirely destroyed. Greater destruction was wrought in the third, and at the end of the second, than the end of the first destruction; the temple was partly rebuilt at the beginning of the second Atlantean epoch.

That temple was an exact counterpart of the Temple on the Heights. It was held in light and glory and the ritual expressed therein was an exact image of the ritual fulfilled in the temple in the etheric worlds of light.

But in this temple the men and women who worshipped there were clothed in the body of flesh, so that the soul, encompassing the glory of the spirit, surrounded by the body of etheric light, was held and encased within the physical body, and certain tests and initiations were undertaken by those who were training for the priesthood, in addition to the tests taken by the priests in the Temple of the first epoch.

For in the second epoch we see them clothed in the body of flesh, a body difficult to handle, difficult to understand, and needing to be fed with physical food, therefore bringing many problems to the leaders of the temple.

The central temple was a vast, circular building, and around the temple itself an outer court, or pathway built of the same stone as the inner temple, with archways above it, sheltered from wind and rain and divided from the inner temple itself by hangings of tapestry and woven material.

This courtyard was not unlike that part of your cathedral Church known as the cloisters, and opening from it were twelve subsidiary temples – the Temple of Light, the Temple of Sound, the Temple of Colour, the Temple of the Law of God, the Temple of Preparation, the Temple of Science, the Temple of Culture, the Temple of the Outside World, and four other temples.

The number of priests and novices working in this temple was considerably more than those required in some of the later Egyptian temples, and although there were a large number of Master-Initiate Priests, they appeared infrequently, for at this stage they were only just beginning to become clothed in the physical body; they still held the etheric glory of the coat of skin; therefore they did not appear in the public worship of the temple at this time, except on special occasions set apart for this particular worship.

The highpriest of the temple, working under the guidance and direction of these Master-Initiates, held for his serving two lesser priests, and these lesser priests were of quite a different order from the highpriest; they could, therefore, never become highpriest. Their training and their testing for the positions they held were severe. The one was called the student and the other the bard, and these words still hold in all Druid ceremonies today. The student stood at the right hand of the highpriest and the bard upon the left. Their duty was to hold the etheric cloak which encompassed the highpriest during his ministry in the temple.

Beyond the temple there stretched the Garden of God, the garden known as the Garden of Remembrance, through which you pass during the hours of sleep and where you meet

60

your friends who are waiting for you there after the change called death. This garden is planted with the trees from which the workers in the temple receive their names.

It is a garden tended and beautiful, with fair lawns surrounding the temple itself and paths of that iridescent stone, of which the temple is built, which can be bent and moulded by the power of spirit passing through the hands of the workman, but can never be broken, and which becomes destruction in the shape of fire when it is hit with a heavy hammer or tool.

Fair rivers flow through the gardens, cool blue waters, where those who served the temple could rest and meditate and fulfil their own mental service by themselves.

On one side of the temple lay the Valley where dwelt those people who, when and as they became ready, were levitated to the temple.

But on the other side of the hill was a very different picture, a rough, wild hillside, with harsh crags, and beyond this hill, as far as the eye could see, a valley with dark, dense trees of jungle growth, in which creatures lived who as yet would seem to have no connection with the temple itself.

Pre-eminent among these creatures was an animal which resembled the swine. They were harmless, but they dwelt in vast dark herds, moving together with swiftness through the undergrowth, snuffling the ground with an almost unbearable sound, filthy in their habits and caring nothing for shelter or covering of any sort. They fed on the husks which fell from the trees of the valley. And here you have the symbol for the parable of the Prodigal Son, great dark beasts, and aeons of time before the second destruction of Atlantis there came to the temple a great darkness, a darkness begot originally of jealousy and pride of place and the desire to supersede his fellow man, by those who were training as the lesser priests.

They sought to explore the crags and rocks of the great hill and also the great dark forests, though these were forbidden to them by the discipline of the temple. They rejected this discipline and grew discontented and ill-at-ease. For this they suffered the punishment meted to them by the highpriest in a special concourse in the Temple, a concourse when the

61

Master Initiates dwelt in the great Sleep and, journeying in the place of light, returned bringing back to the highpriest who ministered at the altar the words of God, that these children of men should be chastened and should learn of the Law of God, and they obeyed it.

But they grew in number, and there came a day when they went forth during the night season at the time of the full moon of May, which you call today the Wesak Moon. They journeyed forth from the Temple and rested the night in the Garden of God, thinking thereby to draw from the garden the power, the strength and the light which God gave to man for his upbuilding.

Throughout the whole history of that second Atlantean temple missionaries were sent forth twelve at a time to the valley which lay through the gardens on the other side of the temple, and you have the counterpart of that in the sending forth of the Disciples. If you study the words of the Master Jesus which precede and follow the sending forth of His Disciples, you will realise what a clear picture you are given of His determination to follow out the principle of the Atlantean Temple.

When the morning came, those who had gone forth in anger felt no refreshment from their night in the Garden of God. Yet they rose and went forth, and descending the hill ventured to the borders of the great jungle and called forth from that jungle mighty beasts who should help them to hew and prepare the stone with which they wanted to build their temple.

The highpriest called to them. They heard him but answered not; they placed a veil between themselves and him, that his voice might not reach them, and they continued their labour until on the side of that great cliff, greater than any cliff you have ever seen in your country, built of dark grey stony crag, there rose a building, strange in structure, built on eight pillars.

No stone walls surrounded the pillars. It was open, this lower temple, to the light of day, to the wind and sunshine. It was built on the dark side of the valley.

The temple itself, builded after the manner of the workers of darkness, was one great chamber, at the east end of which were separated three smaller chambers.

When the building was complete the makers of darkness returned, first to the Garden of God, then to the temple. The highpriest knew they were coming and he called the priests together that they should build a circle of light round the temple itself.

Around the temple were the cloisters and in these cloisters he bade the makers of darkness wait. They waited for the passing of many moons. They were impatient, but the highpriest called them not for they wished to tell him that they had built a temple in which the beasts of the forest could rest and find shelter and shade.

The highpriest knew their hearts and saw that there was another purpose altogether in this strange temple they had built; and he called to them in the silence to repent and speak truth. But they would not.

Among the temple servants there was one called As Judah, and he it was who was guardian of the western door of the temple which faces the great High Altar. The leader of the makers of darkness went to As Judah and he made him many promises, promises of high place of power and pomp and ceremony.

As Judah stood aside at a moment when the chief of the makers of darkness placed his hand upon the latch of the door, and the makers of darkness entered the Temple of Light.

The veils descended, though at this time the Master-Initiates were absent, and the veils glowed and glistened and light was drawn from them towards the makers of darkness.

The highpriest called to them that they might hear his voice speak the word of God, to leave their ways in the darkened valley. But they would not, and when they went forth they were cut off from the Temple of Light, that they might go their own way in the darkened valley.

The priests of the Temple of Light passed many days of fasting and abstinence and prayer within the temple, until the highpriest's voice was heard by As Judah, and he came forth and confessed in the bitter pain of his heart that he had betrayed the Father-Mother God, the Lord God whom he had served.

The highpriest said, 'Go thou forth. As Judas shalt thou be

known. Through all time shalt thou appear and thy spirit shall wander in the waste places of the earth until thou hast expiated the grievous wrong which thou hast done the Lord High God.''

And Judas went forth sorrowful, and when he would enter the Garden of God an invisible wall stood before him, and when he would descend the garden of blossoms to the valley of light, an invisible wall barred his way. The only place he could find peace was by the flowing waters of the great river.

The great dark temple existed for aeons of time, going its darkened way, ever covering the light and glory of the Temple of Light, and numbers of people from the beauteous side of the valley came and joined them and there was magic done therein and the darkness of ugly things in the name of God, but in reality under the name of Satanaku, for Satanaku governed the creatures which dwelt in the darkened jungle.

Those who ministered in the darkened temple were hungered. They were not desirous to work; they did not grow or prepare the food. The great fruits gave of their milk to the Temple on the Tableland, the great trees grew where the servants of the Lord High God gathered the fruits and gave them to the temple service. Therefore, they sought their food elsewhere, and in seeking that food they sought to take life and they took the life of the creatures of the darkened valley, and strange as it was, the more life they took the more these creatures multiplied, until there came a day when they decided that they would worship a god of their own. They set up an image of the great creatures that had assisted in the building of their temple, and in worshipping that god they poured out the life of the lesser creatures as their sacrifice.

Only portions of that sacrifice were eaten by the priests for their daily food and great portions of it were cast aside in that land which lay between that temple and the great darkened valley, and the swine came from the darkened jungle and devoured the remnants of the feast.

Those who ministered in the dark temple increased in number and the highpriest of the Temple of Light knew that the design in building the temple of pillars was that through apertures in the temple walls itself, the ritual in the Temple of

64

Light could be observed, and with much prayer and fasting he beseeched the Father-Mother God that a wall of ether should be placed between the Temple of Light and the Temple of Darkness. This, by the word of God, was done.

Yet those in the temple of darkness sought ever more and more power for themselves. They sought to build a bigger temple. They sought to harness the creatures of the valley to their service. Above all, they desired to destroy the great Temple of Light which now no longer could they see from their own temple walls.

They worked magic while asleep and it was the sleep of a trance condition, not a trance for spiritual purposes but a condition of the very ugliest and darkest texture into which they called the services of the great beasts of the valley, that they should give them of their power for the manifestation of spirits. In order to draw that power from the Temple of Light, the major members of the dark temple called into silence all those who served and placed them in a deep trance sleep, a sleep which called the creatures from the jungle till they completely surrounded the temple on all sides and gave of their power for the manifestation of darkness.

In that trance state there was visualised the Temple of Light, the Master-Initiates asleep behind the veils, that sleep in which they journeyed to the place of God and brought back the purpose of His will for man.

The power of the temple of darkness was greater than any power of light that had existed towards the end of the second period of Atlantis.

Those in the darkened temple took from the highpriest Initiates their sleep so that they could no longer journey in their soul-spirit to the place of light. Then their spirits fell and their light was dim and the physical body knew them no more, for the Father-Mother God rewarded His own and He released the highpriest Initiates from the bodies of flesh that they might dwell for ever beside Him in the place of light.

When the release was completed the Father God commanded that the continent should be destroyed. First sent He the fire and after the fire the whirlwind, and after the whirlwind the tempest and after the tempest the flood.

65

CHAPTER NINE

The Destruction of Atlantis

We are conscious at all times when our thoughts dwell upon Atlantis of a deep peace and harmony – not a lazy, or indolent spirit but a spirit of life, pulsating, strong and free. We are conscious of people who – their soul and personality one in unity of love and understanding – seek the good of their fellowmen and who seek to make life beautiful by the cultivation of beauty in the temple and of greater beauty even in the still peace behind the curtains which covered the altar; of beauty of form and dress, beauty of work and service; until the power of the dark temple grew and increased.

Now the rites in the dark temple were held in the same way and at the same hours as the rites in the Temple of Light except for one point, and that was that the Temple of Light and all who worked and served therein found their greatest force and power at the time of the full moon, whereas those who worked and served in the temple of darkness found their greatest force and light at the time of the new moon. You will find, those of you who heal today, that when you are touching a soul which has been partly, or wholly accustomed to the temple of darkness in Atlantis, that the heart and the mind will open out to you better on the new moon than on the full moon. You cannot judge when you first confer with such a patient but you will come to feel the vibration and to realise that the heart of your patient beats more smoothly and more easily at the time of the moon to which it belongs.

The rites in the dark temple increased and there came a voice from Heaven which commanded that a great gathering of the priests and the servants of the temple should take place within the Temple of Light, that the ornaments of precious metal should be placed upon the altar, and the altar decked as for a high festival – and it was done. And behind the altar, in the little chamber adorned for the sowing of the seed, there came together those who should eventually lead the Temple of Light in the day of Aquarius. Within the temple on this occasion when all was hushed and still, when the doors were shut and the guardians of the temple crossed their halberds across the doors that none might enter, the Lord God spoke to the assembled multitude.

Now you must know the difference between God the Father, Father-Mother, and the Lord God; the Lord God is the ruler of the planet – it is He who interprets the Will of the Father-Mother God to those who are called to serve Him.

And the Lord God entered, in the spirit, the Temple on the Heights and He commanded the workers in wood, the craftsmen in metal, the workers in stone and the craftsmen in precious silks and materials, that they should each and severally draw together and place themselves in the form of triangles throughout the temple. And He called forth one – Horhetep – from among those who served the temple and served the temple in a very unusual way, for to him was given the work of organising the place of the servants of the temple and the work that they should do therein. He, it was, who saw that the temple was cleansed and purified; that the stones, glistening in the sunshine, were kept bright and true, who saw into the hearts of the servants of the temple and knew when one should be stood aside and not permitted to continue.

Again the temple doors were barred from within, that none might hear the voice of the Lord God when He spoke. And He commanded that three ships should be built and these ships should be known as the Arks. The Ark of the Covenant of the Lord, the Ark of the Servants of the Lord, and the Ark of the World of Creatures. Because of their great power and holiness the records of the first two Arks have not yet been disclosed, so that the only story which has come to you through your Bible

67

is the story of the Ark which bore the animals to the dry land from the place of torment.

The Ark of the Covenant of the Lord was builded in a strange and wonderful way. In the very centre of the ship there was a temple, a temple built entirely of the tree which is called the shittim tree in the Bible but is known to you as a kind of acacia; the wood of the shittim tree polished by hand, was inlaid with the wood of many other trees, and above all, a band of wood from the tulip tree surrounded each portion of the temple, the lintels of the doors and the doors themselves. Again, this wood was polished by hand without colour or pigment of any description. This inner temple was exceeding small, only large enough to contain a minute altar, and beneath the altar, covered in with rich silks, the chest which contained the vessels of the altar service.

The end of Atlantis was a destruction of great darkness. The destruction was not of all men who served the temple, for there were some of the great highpriests who had not given themselves to the blood sacrifices, nor had they demeaned themselves with ill behaviour in the temple, nor had they defamed the temple, or ruined its appointments and its hangings. These men, astrologers all, foreseeing the coming destruction, on the instructions of the Father-Mother God, were withdrawn into a great white building attached to the temple but enclosed and apart from it. It was they who knew the moment of the final destruction and were able to read in the stars the long period of darkness which would ensue; it was at their command, under the command of the Father-Mother God that a lesser Ark was built, this time of the wood which you know as oak, and in that Ark there were confined all those servants of the temple who, leaving the temple on the advice of the Astrologers, were drawn together in that secret place and were therefore ready to go out towards the Light.

The strange thing about this secret place was that it was entirely invisible to the workers of darkness within the temple. Attached to the temple where the darkness was being wrought, was this minute and beautiful building wrought of marble of many colours, enthroned with Light in which there dwelt and served Beings who linked with the greatest force of God

Himself, who were not empowered or bidden by God to give any power for the depletion of the darkness in the temple itself, but only to pursue their own tasks in teaching and training their astrological students, in preparing a room for the weavers that they should build exquisite hangings of silk, and wrought gold and silver for the temple to which they were later to be guided.

In the great area of Atlantis which lay beyond the garden and between the temple itself and the valley, wrought the craftsmen day and night to build the three arks to the specification given over the ether by the highest highpriest, an instrument for the voice of God working under the direction of God and fulfilling His plan.

The Lord God appointed Horhetep in charge of the Ark of the Servants of the Lord – and Noami in charge of the Ark of the World of Creatures.

The Lord God departed, having laid his hands in blessing upon the head of Horhetep and commanded him that in the great spaces of the forest, covers should be erected that the workmen might work speedily and well in the building of the ships.

Two moons later the same ceremony in the temple took place and again Horhetep was called forth by the Lord God who commanded him to prepare a fleet of small ships which should be rode in the water with tools of wood. He gave to Horhetep – by the mouth of the highpriest – the names of all those who were worthy and ready to occupy those ships when the moment came for the temple to be destroyed. Between those two periods when the Lord God spoke in the Temple, the Lord God caused to be tested all those whose names were called that they might be ready and pure and clean, untouched by the Temple of Darkness.

Those who worked within the Temple of Darkness under Eranus, or Satanaku, approached slowly and gradually to the Temple of Light, mentally and physically undermining the foundation. Tremendous forces were on the way and they came, and while the craftsmen and the workers in wood prepared the ships in the great corners of the forest, they were surrounded by the Lord God with clouds of mist, that none should see their work or count their ways, or satisfy their curiosity as to what was being done.

On one great feast day – about the time of Whit Sunday in your calendar – the Lord God again called all whom He had chosen to the Temple of Light and this time a curtain of mist was spread round the Temple of Light completely excluding it from the view of those who moved outside it. And the watcher came down from the temple roof and holding high the wand of office he led Horhetep up the winding stairs and the craftsmen and the servants and the workers and the worshippers in the temple who had been chosen for the work of the Father-Mother God to be saved from the destruction of Atlantis – they mounted the staircase to within the cupola of the temple itself, and held their service there.

There they waited; they fasted, they were silent, and the watcher from the tower saw the water rising; the earth was shaken with mighty rockings and the clouds darkened the sun and the moon became as blood; remember, the moon represented the blood sacrifices which never ceased by now in the Temple of Darkness. And the swine came up from the valley, feeling the rising of the elements and afraid, and the people of the valley were sore troubled and trembled; and the people of the temple waited in silence and fasting.

As the waters rose till they covered the trees of the forest, there came forth one of these great covered ships; Noami and his family stood at the prow and they opened the door and the creatures ready and waiting moved into the ship; the doors were shut and the ship moved away over the waters.

So there went forth first of all down the great and glorious river of Light the Ark of the Creatures, and these creatures did not have to be collected for they were ready; in their twos, they came in perfect order, walking, directed by the power of God, acknowledging in their own simple hearts the voice of God, moving slowly through the great forest to the river bank, where they were enclosed in the Ark as the first great drops of water fell from the sky.

The symbol which was carved on the prow was the man with the pitcher of water, the sign of Aquarius. As the ship moved away a few great drops of rain fell and lo! there came

70

forth – again surrounded by the mist of the Lord – the second ship and into this ship entered Horhetep and the high priests, the secondary priests and the lesser priests and the boys and girls who were engaged in the service of the Temple, but leaving behind them all those who had composed the triangles in the temple at the command of the Lord God.

The second Ark contained those who were called upon to build the new service in the new temple, in the new land and these were enthroned at the time of the full moon, and the light of the moon shone dim and white upon their pathway. The pathway led them down the hill towards the river and in the distance they could see the Ark of the Creatures moving slowly, gently and peaceably away on the waters.

A great cloud appeared to surround the ship and the voice of the Lord God pierced through the cloud giving directions to Horhetep, showing him above the mists which surrounded him a great and mighty figure with the body of a lion, the wings of an eagle, and the head of a man. And the Lord God bade Horhetep to lead forth the Servants of the Lord, trust himself upon the waters and follow the Ark of Noami.

The third Ark, to the music of the lyre, moved down the great river into the sunrise; the Ark of the Covenant of the Lord, the Ark which contained the Holy Place wherein the sacred writings were held. The priests within the silent subsidiary temple knew from the sound of the waters that it was time to leave, and they formed a group moving away from the altar and from the small chamber behind the altar down the central aisle of the temple to the doorway. The doorway did not open, for these Beings of Light knew no obstacle. They moved through the doorway on to the path at a moment when the orgies in the great temple were at their ugliest and the cries of those who were sacrificed were almost unendurable, knowing it was the will of God and that the moment had been reached when they were no longer allowed to give light to the great temple of Atlantis. They moved out, covered with a cloud of light through which no man would see them, no being would see them, no creature of darkness would see them, and on to the great Ark of the Covenant where each intuitively knew his place and took it in silence. The waters, cooperating

71

in the work of God, moved the Ark of the Covenant from the bank till it entered the centre of the great river of light and moved out behind the other two.

Those who served in this Ark of the Covenant, who were called to prepare the new temple in the new land, where Beings of Light created by God in full adulthood, descending on Rays of Light to their place of service in the temple from which they were so soon to be drawn and from which they were so soon to be taken.

Out of the mists came the boats and into these boats upon dry land stepped all who were called to be worthy servants of the Father-Mother God and the voice of the Lord God commanded them where they should sit and how they should row and in which direction they should guide their boats. They moved forth in the mists created by the Lord God for their protection; none who were left on Atlantis knew that they had gone.

The earth rocked and shook and broke asunder and the lightning cut in half the great trees of the forest; the gardens in their great beauty with their wondrous perfume were destroyed by the floods and rain, rain so strong that the rivers overflowed, rain so strong that it churned the soil of the valley into mud, and the mud rose with the water and the earth cracked and groaned under the terrific force of the Lord God's power, power given to Him for this act of destruction, that the darkness should be cleared away from the world which God had made.

As they sailed forth upon the waters they watched the temple heave and rock under the stress of the storm, they watched the earth crack and the Temple break asunder and disappear. They sailed forth for many days, Horhetep holding always within his vision the Ark of Noami which held the animals of Atlantis itself. So guided was he that he knew that when the dove went forth from the Ark and came back with the olive branch, it was the symbol which the Lord God had promised He would send him, when He described the great beast of stone which Horhetep was commanded to superintend in his new country for the building for all time of the symbol of the Lord. The Voice of the Lord God continually spoke to Horhetep from within the cloud and He told him to sail until the dove in its wisdom bringing back the olive leaves, showed them that they were already far from the Atlantean Continent and approaching a new land. The Lord God told Horhetep that this land would be a land of many waters, many branches of one river which would run through fertile land and where the people who Horhetep loved and guided would find rest and peace.

So progressed they through a mighty blue sea and the whole of their sailing was calm until the cloud which surrounded them and hid them from sight departed and showed them the Delta of the River Nile, the many branches of the river, the untouched soil beyond it. Horhetep saw that the words of the Lord God had been true indeed and he looked for a city to dwell in whose name and foundations are God.

The land that rose out of mud and slime was a long distance from the original continent of Atlantis. For a while the Father-Mother God remained aloof from this darkened land, and because wherever there is mud and slime there will be life of an animal nature, creatures began to live in the muddy waters, creatures, some of them which remained in the waters themselves, others moved out on the top of the waters till they found somewhere where they could rest, and there grew reptiles, worms, serpents of all descriptions, and finally the great beasts that you know as the prehistoric animals. This is the first record, for the records of the Temple of Light are not yet revealed.

A long period of time elapsed and then there appeared other animals, which in turn gave place to creatures which were the forerunners of the people of Lemuria, great apes and monkeys, hairless for many generations. Then the male-female element and the creation of sex became a part of the history of Lemuria. The men and women who represented this land were almost inhuman in their ugliness, their distorted features, their coarse scaly skin, their arms which finished at the wrist to which were no palms or fingers, their feet which were stumps moving about in the mud, and gradually as the mud subsided and became solid and hard, the need for feet manifested and these creatures grew feet, and later the need

73

for hands and they grew hands, at first with only a thumb and no fingers, and later the need for individual fingers arose and the hands were grown the same shape but very much coarser than those you see today.

It was a land of great darkness, great ugliness, because sex was at its ugliest and worst attitude that it had ever been known to exist; even today there is no darkness like the darkness of that Lemurian land, although many lands and many continents have passed through great periods of unbelief and immorality which accompany always the development of sex among those who do not recognise or realise the power of God.

And these creatures knew nothing about God, had no idea of God; they had been created out of the mud and the slime and the ugliness of destruction. At the same time as this form of creation was going forward a great Light was spreading in the land which became known as Khemu, and later Egypt. There great temples were being built, beautiful creatures were roaming the deserts and the wilderness and peopling the rivers. A great Light, suffused at the dawn but breaking forth, was bringing into incarnation once again the great Beings of Light born to full adulthood in the great temples.

These Beings were endowed with speech, but not with speech as you know it, for their voices were musical tones and vibrations, such as you would call notes today, each note representing a sound, each sound and combination of sounds representing the necessary phrase. Very few sounds were necessary. These were Beings of Light who understood each other by the movement of the lips and the gestures of the hands, the movement of the eyes and the colour of the eyes, and the eternal moving vibrations of Light which passed through the aura. For one could look at another and receive a ray of Light which gave consent to the plan in his mind, and another could look at the aura and receive a ray of Light which set aside another plan in his mind. And always creeping closer and closer was the influence of the Lemurian continent, for these strange creatures were evolving, evolving to a point when they developed minds which desired to serve.

Finally, there came a moment when the continent of

Lemuria was also destroyed under the waters; but this time the Lord God planted a garden, and where there had been ugliness and despair he brought joy and Light, and those who had brought the third Ark to the Land of Khemu brought also plants and seeds, they journeyed again and they scattered the seeds for the good of the Lemurian land, and the slime and the mud began to vanish and a great soil eruption occurred. And instead of the darkness of a volcanic eruption the eruption was of soil which would grow all that was given to it to grow.

The first Lemurians to leave the darkness and to be drawn towards this new land of Light were those who tended the soil and built gardens and planted seeds and grew trees, planted tubers and grew blossoms and other tubers, and grew food which was suitable for man to eat.

As soon as a garden was there, our Lord God called to Himself those by whom He had been commanded and asked if all things were good, and the Father-Mother God saw that it was good and began His work of the new creation. And into that creation there came the two Beings whom you know as Adam and Eve, Beings who had known in their hearts the darkness of Lemuria and loathed it and were anxious to escape from it, and knew also the secret of sex and the purpose of this new creation of the Father-Mother God – that man should bring life into the world by his own efforts. Thus, once again, a great garden was created under the guidance of the Lord God, under the guidance of the Father-Mother God, for the habitation of created man. The first Beings into whom our Father-Mother God had breathed the breath of creative life, had been given by Him the great living soul itself, the soul which eventually manifested the personality, and began the simple, easygoing, happy life of the wayfaring man. For the wayfaring man to you means a beggar, a gipsy, a nomad, but to us who touch that word in your service and your ministry, it means the first man who learned to till the soil, to love the trees and the growing things, to use the plants of the earth for his well being and his food and to create life among the creatures, and bring the creatures to his service, also under the command of the Lord God, under the command of the Father-Mother God and in the name of the Father-Mother God Himself.

CHAPTER TEN

The Building of the Pyramid

A time came before the destruction of Atlantis when the Atlantean Masters left the Temple on the Heights and went forth to found a new race of men in Khemu, the country we now call Egypt, for they, with the artificers and the workers in precious metal and the workers in wood and stone and the architects and designers, were sent forth to a barren desert long before the Flood. Those who have visited the Pyramids will know that round their base there have been discovered many seashells, proving that they were complete, at least outside, before the coming of the Flood which brought those great ships carrying the animals and the trees and the plants and the servants of the temple, who were ready and able to found a new kingdom in the name of God and to preserve their great teaching for the moment when God's hand alone would open the Recording Temple and give His wisdom to the world.

Among these highpriests of Atlantis was the Master who is known to you as Thoth of the Egyptians. He was the scribe of the Gods, and when the command of our Father-Mother God went forth from the Temple of Atlantis that these Masters should gather together and go forth into Egypt, or Khemu, it was Thoth who took down the commands of God in writing, who preserved those commands upon Papyrus, and who was responsible for that great and wonderful chamber in the centre at the top of the Pyramids where these sacred writings are preserved to this day. Heat cannot touch them, water cannot touch them, the hand of man cannot touch them; for they are the work of Thoth, the Scribe of the Gods.

King Solomon was a man of peace, gentle of disposition, with the vision of God within his soul, and his clairvoyant vision was attuned to the highest possible vibration of life. It was Solomon who commanded a Master, whose name in the time of King Solomon was Hiram Abiff, to build his Great Temple. But it was Thoth, the scribe, who issued the measurements and the plans for the great temples of the Pyramids. There has been much conjecture as to how those stones were carried, how they were cut with the primitive tools in use in those days, how they were placed together so that the joins in them cannot be seen. Many other questions rise to our lips when we stand before these gigantic buildings and realise, breathlessly almost, that they are the work of man. Yes, they are the work of man but the work of man guided by God, held by God in obedience, in service and in wisdom. For the great Atlantean Master, who was the Leader of the highpriests of Atlantis, brought with him from that mighty Temple the great Stone Shamir; for the stone always forms the foundation of man's material life and the symbol of his spiritual life.

The plans which were drawn by Thoth were mirrored in the Stone Shamir, for the stone was softly and gently moved over the drawings which had been made under the guidance of God himself for the building of the Pyramid.

When the work of the Stone had been blessed in its service over the plans, the Stone was placed into position on the great granite rocks which had been brought from a great distance for the building of the Pyramid. The Stone Shamir makes no mistake; patiently, and with success, the stones fell apart and they fell soundlessly at the information given by Thoth, as the Word of God was that the Temple should be built without sound of a hammer, chisel, or anvil, exactly the same way as you read of the building of the Temple of King Solomon. No sound was heard. So the Great Pyramid was carven in stone by the sacred Stone Shamir, and two sets of staircases were set within it. The one staircase was the path of the novice down into the very bowels of the earth, to take his tests for initiation, and the other staircase led up, up, through the great Pyramid's centre, to the secret chamber where the records of the wisdom of God and the building of the Temple of the glory of Atlantis, of the journey from Atlantis to found the work of God in a new land, were all held in sacred records till the moment that the voice of God shall bid the Pyramid to be opened and the records revealed to the sight and ears of those who are ready and able to accept the wisdom of God.

The three highpriests spent many hours in this hidden chamber. They climbed the great staircase on foot without fatigue, as all men climb in life who have the Spirit of God within them, and even Pharaoh, who could never be refused admittance, must climb that staircase blindfold and stand within the record chambers blindfold, for he may not know the future which God has prepared for man, nor may he know the past.

We journey towards that moment when those records will be opened and those with the eyes of the spirit ready, the ears of the spirit attuned and the heart of the spirit a sacred flame of love, shall have revealed to them the past, the present and the future.

Thoth reincarnated in Egypt in due course of incarnation as I-em-Hotep, the Healer highpriest of the Temple of Isis.

CHAPTER ELEVEN

The Temple of the North

When that wonderful Temple of Atlantis was to suffer the last and final destruction, three covered boats, with a large fleet of open boats, sailed from the land.

At this time, our Father-Mother God had chosen those who went forth from Atlantis with great care and circumspection and with understanding of the needs of those who landed eventually in Egypt, touching that rich fertile valley uncultivated with that great river flowing towards the sea by many mouths.

First, Horhetep – under the instruction of Ptah – on what would be today the outskirts of Cairo built and founded the great Temple of the North and later he built the great Sphinx out of solid blocks of marble. This was carried out under the instruction of angelic beings and was so arranged that it was the entrance to the Temple of the North. Although this entrance later became closed, and later kings of Egypt built many Sphinx and pyramids for mausoleums for their own body, yet there was always beneath the sand the entrance to the great Temple of the North in which the Neophytes dedicated to the priesthood should take their initiation.

When the outward semblance and structure of the Temple of the North was completed, Horhetep received instructions to build the Temple of the South and the men who had carried and carved the stone for the Temple of the North, the artisans and the craftsmen, the workers in precious metal, the weavers of silk, were diverted from the Temple of the North, with the blessing of the Father-Mother God and were directed to build the Temple of the South. Those who remained in the Temple of the North smoothed and prepared the stones of the floors, hanging the rich textures upon the walls, digging deep into the heart of the temple where the initiation should take place.

From time to time in this life you must touch sudden memories, sudden inner feelings of linking within that Temple, with the experiences through which you pass in your dedication which link with the initiation of the neophyte.

At the time appointed for the neophyte to be presented for initiation, he would present himself at the entrance to a long causeway, his parents would stand, one on the right and one on the left, two feet behind him, and as the priest came down the causeway to take the neophyte towards the temple, the parents knelt and blessed him on his way, then turned aside and departed from him.

Although the description of what followed takes only a few moments of time, the initiation of a neophyte occupied a very long period of time. It was a matter conducted with circumspection, great understanding, and great ceremony, but ceremony of a very simple nature, which links with the temples which are being founded in the world of men today, that you may be recalled in memory to that walk up the causeway beside the priest of the Temple of the North and remember also the various incidents which followed.

At the end of the causeway the neophyte reached the door; he was handed over to another priest who already awaited him. You will notice that there was never any signal given, the priest who met the neophyte at the end of the causeway arrived there at the moment he arrived with his parents; the priest meeting the neophyte and the priest at the entrance to the temple were there at the moment that they arrived. The temple doors were not worked by hand, they were moved to open and close by the powerful thought of the priest himself; yet, although concentrating upon these details, he never forgot his duty towards the neophyte, nor the explanation which must be given.

The neophyte was then conducted by the second priest into

a large chamber at the entrance to the temple, where the body was unclothed of the garments of earth and completely cleansed and purified with water blessed in the temple itself. The head and the hands, the palms of the hands, and the heart were anointed; no other part of the body was anointed, and in the anointing oil the symbol of the sacred ankh was wrought upon the chest of the neophyte, before he was clad in a garment of white linen reaching to the ground, covering the body completely, but leaving the head uncovered. The priest then placed two small feathers intertwined in the hair of the neophyte symbolising that he was now ready for spiritual preparation and spiritual purification before he entered the service of the temple.

The neophyte was then handed over to another priest who took him to a small chapel at the side of the temple. You will notice that the water of the well of purification was at the west end of the temple, the end farthest from the east and where the altar was placed; and the baptismal font in your churches today takes their place from that ancient Temple of the North. And here, within this quiet chamber, a higher priest came and here was the neophyte tested and questioned, great emphasis being laid on the fact that if he would serve God in the temple he must completely and entirely renounce and stamp upon the self. The priest then left him in prayer.

Then came forward two more priests who placed over his eyes a bandage, so that he could not see and taking him by the arms, holding the arms beneath the elbows, they directed his steps down the long passage, down the still longer staircase of stone, into the central chamber of initiation. Here they left him, handing into his hand a small lamp, which he was called upon to hold high in the right hand, in order to be able to discover what manner of chamber it was in which he found himself. He would hear their sandalled feet upon the step, he would hear the great door shut behind them and realise that he was alone, that, in a few moments the flickering flame of the lamp, material light transmuted into the lamp of the spirit, would leave him in total darkness.

If he were right for initiation he would remain very still and be conscious of a strange alertness of mind and consciousness, an alertness which acted as an illumination in the temple itself; he would step forward and back, touching always walls yet knowing that the thing which he sought was the altar of Osiris/Isis and that the altar was surrounded by a lake upon which floated the sacred lotus, which none but the priest might touch.

Fatigued, weary, overcome by a strange drowsiness which comes very often to mediums before a great trial or undertaking, he would lay himself down upon the stone floor and fall asleep. When he woke he realised that the walls on either side contained statues in little alcoves, that if he was to walk without falling, he must take the straight path to the lake and the altar which lay before him. He remembered the explanation given to him by the priest, of the Sphinx which was designed with the body of a lion, that the neophyte should have the strength of the lion to overcome the animal nature of man; he would remember that the priest had said that the head of the Sphinx was the head of a man, the centre of the headdress pointing to the heavens to remind all who saw it that man is spirit, and joined to God can overcome the darkness of the world.

These thoughts passing through his mind enabled him to walk straight forward without fear, till his feet touched the rim of the pool and looking down he saw that every lily was aglow with light and tiny members of the Deva Kingdom had attached to his ankle strings and cords to guide him on the next part of his path.

He turned to the right and passed through a door which opened as he reached it – again by the thought force of the priest in the temple above who guided his steps and watched. Then he found himself in a vast chamber where priests came forward to kneel before him and accept him as one who had been strong enough to set aside the temptations of the world, to conquer his inner self and to touch the light of the spirit, as one should who serves the Father-Mother God.

Into a small chamber on the right he was led. The bandage over his eyes was no longer there. He was disrobed of the white garment and robed in the garment of the priest, with a chain round the neck, from which hung the sacred ankh, the symbol of the key to the mysteries. This was not all, for the ankh could not be used as a key, it was merely a symbol prepared in wax which the student must hold inviolate, until he had the right to kneel at the feet of the highpriest and, rendering the waxen ankh, receive the golden key which opened the door to the inner mysteries of God.

You will, perhaps, remember some point which we have touched upon; it is possible even now that some of your dreams awakening from the subconscious mind bring you pictures of the statues in the underground chamber; it is possible that from time to time you see the lotus blossom and realise the glory of the light of the spirit, as you emerge from the darkness of earth. It is not the first time that you have been helped to face these tests of initiation; you may remember further details if you concentrate upon the picture and fill in, each in its right place, the detail which belongs.

We are here to live in the present on the memories of the past and the vision of the future. In the place of silence, down that long flight of stone steps, where you feel completely alone and deserted, your eyes are bandaged so that only the mirror of the Sphinx is before them, where your feet are almost afraid to go forward – there, and there alone, will you come to the knowledge of the mysteries, in such a way that you may be considered true and strong enough to hold within your hand the sacred ankh, which opens the door for all time.

CHAPTER TWELVE

The Initiation of the Neophyte I

After the neophyte had received the golden key, he was greeted by yet another priest wearing a simple white robe; no symbols, or bands on the hair, no ornament whatsoever, but in his hand a short staff the head of which was the blossom of the lotus. This priest led him into another circular chamber – again the door opened at the thought of the priest, again the door closed as the thought of the priest commanded it – and the student was led forward, where a very simple ritual was performed, showing him that he was now to be dedicated to the Priesthood of Osiris/Isis. He was placed on a low stool – a stool whose reproduction you have seen in many forms since then – it is semi-circular, the stool itself being lower in the middle than the sides and when turned over upside down the legs form also a semi-circle. Here, the neophyte was served with the juice of the pomegranate as a drink, and a wafer, which was placed upon his tongue, as food, the food and drink being the symbol of Osiris/Isis his twinship.

Here, again, the neophyte was asked to pray, and an invisible choir of many voices surrounded the priest and the neophyte; neither joined in the singing, but both were conscious that the atmosphere was filled with colour and movement as well as sound. From alcoves at the side of the chamber there came forth four servants of the Sanctuary, each carrying a portion of the new robe which the student must now don, and in his hands were placed the symbols of power, truth and life – not material power – the power of the world – but spiritual power, for now, as a fully dedicated Priest of Osiris/Isis, he had the power to heal, to conduct the services in the great temples and to kneel in obeisance in the Temple of Osiris/Isis.

He was conducted thrice round the circular chamber, and the third time he reached an alcove near the door where he was reminded of the great office to which he had been admitted, the robe was taken from him, the symbols were handed to another priest, a mysterious door opened and he went through alone to be met on the other side by yet another priest of a different order, behind whom stood twelve sanctuary servants – six carrying bowls of water perfumed with incense and many herbs – six carrying towels of white linen. The neophyte was placed on a hard chair without arms – the symbol of material life and the bare bench on which he would be called upon to sit – and here his hands and his feet were thrice anointed and bathed by the aromatic water held by the servants of the sanctuary, and dried by the servants who held the towels.

When these had disappeared, he was conducted bare-footed into a vast circular chamber, radiant with light and yet not the light of windows, or of the world, for this chamber lay under the third Pyramid and already the neophyte, or priest of Osiris/Isis, had passed underground through that great distance which lies between the first and the third Pyramids of Egypt. In the centre of this magnificent hall there stood a table with four legs – four being the symbol of the square with four sides, which always in Egyptian teaching represents perfection on all planes; the table itself was formed in alabaster and the four legs were the stems of the lotus; the feet, upon which the legs were placed, were the open leaves. Upon this table there stood a very precious jug containing water – the jug being the shape of the lotus bud upon its stem. Beside the jug was a very large bowl shaped as the open blossom of the lotus, the petals curving in slightly; the petals did not touch each other, they were apart, and yet the bowl itself was the form of the perfect blossom – again in shiny alabaster, not the dead white alabaster you so often see on your church altars and pulpits today, but an alabaster of a creamy whiteness, seemingly transfused with the colours of the spectrum – the glaze perfect, the shape of every carved petal also perfect.

The priest spoke – and this was the first time that the priest of Osiris/Isis had heard a voice for a long period for all the other work had been conducted in silence – the priest called attention to the fact that this great chamber was a living lotus blossom, that the heads of the pillars were opening buds, that the blossom which he saw as the empty bowl upon the table was the open blossom, that the jug was again the lotus bud. And he commanded the new priest of Osiris/Isis to pour the water from the jug into the bowl; he explained that the water in the bowl now represented the cosmos and he commanded the young priest to read what he saw in the waters of the great bowl. There were two sessions of vision, one, the movements of the planets, the position of the planets and the stars at that particular moment which they were touching, the position of the stars and the planets at the building of the Sphinx, the position of the stars and the planets at the building of the third Pyramid. All this the young priest did unfalteringly. The priest then passed his right hand slowly round above and over the bowl and commanded the young priest again to observe the pictures in the water, and when that was completed the ministering priest knew that all things were now accomplished and the neophyte could go forth having completed with the utmost perfection the whole of his painful and troublesome initiation.

And yet not all, for no priest could have reached such a point as this without having completed the initiation demanded – now the young priest must face the ordeals. And they were many, and of great importance. And again the priest conducted him to the door which again opened at the thought of the priest and the young priest of Osiris/Isis found himself in a passage whose darkness was so incredible it is something you cannot imagine. He was alone. He stood for a moment; he remembered the sacred lotus and the vision in the bowl; he remembered the bathing of the feet, the presentation of the symbols of power, truth, life; he remembered the long passage; he remembered the moment when he had fallen

86

asleep. Perhaps for a brief second there came to his mind the question of 'how could I be here if I had fallen asleep'; and then he realised, by pausing on the threshold and recovering the memory of the passage he had taken, he had received illumination and the passage before him and around him, although restricted by walls which were very close and left little room for his feet to pass, was radiant with light – the light of the spirit. In his hand was a lamp, not lit with any earthly light but symbolic of the light of the spirit and therefore radiant with light. Steadily he walked to the end of the passage and a voice commanded him to knock – he knocked thrice upon the door, with the knuckle of the middle finger of his right hand and was astonished at the echo such a small tool had created touching the door. The door was opened by a highpriest and behind him four priests, who commanded the young priest to enter, and this time he found himself in a rectangular chamber, the pillars of which were blue. The tops of the pillars were carved with the symbols of Egypt, the flail, the mitre crown, the lotus crown, while the base were carved in the form of the caduceus.

Here the young priest realised suddenly how fatigued he was; he felt he was going to fall and he was borne up by two of the attendant priests and guided to a couch and there he gratefully lay down. To his surprise he opened his eyes and realised that the whole of the experience of initiation had been taken during the period that he had slept, for he was now once again in the circular chamber where he had fallen asleep; he had not noticed the pillars, nor had he noticed the couch, for he was carried at that moment out of the world, so that the experience which he took was the experience of the soul without the body – apart from the personality, apart from the earth – the true experience of initiation.

It is your soul which passes through the tests of initiation. It is the mind, which is the organ of the soul-body that creates anew for you the experience when you wake, and this experience must be transmuted into the power which the brain can handle, so long as your soul is incarnate in the body of earth. You may call it memory, you may call it what you will; one day man will realise that what he learns in the dream state is not only of as great importance as what he learns in the physical body during the ordinary procedure of life but that the one is inseparable from the other, and that the experience which you gain in sleep, based and built upon the experience of your day's work in the world of men, is the true life of the spirit.

CHAPTER THIRTEEN

The Initiation of the Neophyte II

On awaking, the neophyte finds himself alone and power and strength coming to him from a source which he is not conscious of touching. The priest approaches him with food and drink for he has now fasted, partaking neither of solid or liquid food, for seven days; he is not ravenous, nor hungry as if he had fasted, for all the time that he has been undertaking these experiences – he has, to a large extent, been fed by the spirit with light and power – yet he seats himself gratefully and partakes of the nourishment handed to him.

Following the meal he is then introduced to a ritual of cleansing; the priest explains the cleansing carefully and then conducts him to a small grey stone chamber where the experiences of the Hall of Ordeals and all that went with these rituals, are washed away by laving the body in sacred water. Here he dons a robe of white linen, high to the neck, entirely without ornament except for a girdle round the waist, upon which are hanging a golden key and a golden ankh; the golden key signifies that he is now permitted to unlock the mysteries – the hidden mysteries of God containing God's will for man, God's law for man, and the ankh, which is the symbol of truth and justice. And here, kneeling, the priest endows him with the name of Asinrah Ankh, Keeper of the Ankh, Disciple of Osiris.

He then rests upon a couch for he still has another ordeal which must be faced, before he can be introduced to the priest of the temple, and this is the ordeal of suggestion. He must withdraw into a cell-like chamber where he will make his mind completely blank and keep it blank throughout the whole of the experience, and then the armies of Satanaku are brought towards him and he is pressed with thought, tormented with mental vision, disturbed by all that can be given to destroy the silence in which he rests. He remains strong and yet the power of this suggestion is such that he could very easily weaken even after passing all the tests which we have already described. He remains strong, unflinching, concentrated upon the ankh and the key which represent for him the victory over darkness; perhaps he sees himself going forward to unlock another door, to unlock it himself, not to wait while another unlocks this door to the mysteries. But all the time he knows that whatever happens he must remain completely quiescent and hold the light of God within himself, that he may not be disturbed by these demonstrations, strong words, strong impressions, which can turn him and deter him from the path. At the end of this experience he falls into a deep sleep upon the stone floor, and wakes to find himself upon a soft couch with the priest standing beside him, who will conduct him to the highpriest of the temple as one who has passed the first stage of his initiation and wishes to become a temple servant. The highpriest receives him, he holds him by the right hand and leads him up the short flight of steps into the great temple itself; ascending from the darkness the neophyte finds himself almost blinded by the light, for the windows of this temple are in the sloping roof and they hold the light; and the light penetrates the temple itself in great shafts, for this is the light that must guide the student towards the priesthood. It is possible that he feels very pleased with himself, rather, as you would say, on top of the world, ready to build, to accept the service of God without fear or question; he feels a powerful person, one who has come through great and mighty experiences, one who has released his soul from the body to experience all that was necessary in the Place of Light. While he is, in a sense, patting himself upon the back, the priest commands him to kneel upon the stone floor and give thanks.

90

Following the thanksgiving he is taken to a small cell completely bare except for a table and a chair; he has no possessions; he took nothing into the Hall of Experience and he brought nothing out; the white linen robe is laid aside and he is clothed in a black garment from the neck to the feet, tied round the waist with a brown cord upon which a wooden ankh is fixed. He follows the priest into the temple itself and here he is given to understand that he shall perform, for one year and one day, all the menial tasks of the temple and the courtyards surrounding it; he shall set aside his pride, he shall forget that his first thought of being an important person buoyed him up and held him; he shall forget all that, and in his simple black robe and bare feet he shall serve the temple.

For a year we see him, broom in hand, sweeping the steps and the outer courts, down on his knees cleansing the stone flags of the temple floor, never allowed to raise his eyes to the rays of light coming through the windows, or, more important still to him – for this is what he has worked for – to gaze upon the uncovered altar of the Lord our God.

The year is long and during that time, except for a seat at the back of the great temple – the humble seat of a worker in domestic service – he remains apart, hardly spoken to by the novices who are further advanced, hardly recognised by the priests whose place he makes smooth for them; and his hours of leisure are spent in meditation, in conquering the self to such a degree that he can remain completely quiet and listen for the voice of God; and sometimes he feels that the voice is not even near him, taking no note of his experiences. He feels forgotten, cast out.

All that is part of his training for the next step. When he has worked for a year and a day, he is called by the lesser priests of the temple to humble himself, before the uncovered altar of the Lord our God, and here he is given a rough chain of beads around his neck, to show that he has completed his year's work in menial service and can stand upright and look upright at the light pouring through the temple windows. In his right hand is placed a staff, in his left a wooden bowl, and the door of the temple is opened for him and he goes out in the world of men, to serve for a year and a day in the same humble capacity as he has served in the temple but without the strength, the light, the power of the temple behind him. The service that he must take in the world is of the humblest kind, for humility is the great lesson of this stage in his training and preparation for the priesthood; he goes from house to house begging his bread; he fulfils the service of the scavengers in the streets, and only by the growing light in his aura and the light in his eyes can you recognise him as a servant of the temple.

From the moment he leaves the temple door and goes out into the world alone, he is carefully watched by that group of Masters whose work it is to watch all those to whom has been entrusted the golden key – the ankh he carries close about his heart; the key is attached to the girdle of his robe, the girdle of the mendicant priest; and all that is beautiful in life seems to be left behind, during that year in the temple service; he has grown close to the joy of the altar which is now denied him. And how they watch – those unseen Masters – and how they check the completion of each and every task. They stay beside him till he is conscious of their presence and sees the all-guiding influence which strengthens him all the way.

At the end of the year he returns to the temple, his robe has not been changed, it is tattered from its contact with the material world, it is dusty and travel-worn, and his face is seared and marked by the difficulties he has encountered. But he returns with joy, for all those last few trials and difficulties came to him so easily; for the work of the temple lies before him and he knows he is completing a cycle and re-entering the Place of Peace.

The children of Aquarius today begin with the temple service; all the preparation which we call initiation is done in the sleep state; therefore, from the beginning, we must cultivate that ability to meditate and to retire into the silence, for in that lies our strength. If during each day of twenty four hours we keep one brief half-hour for our link with God, we shall find our strength growing until it is sufficient to conquer the numerous and sometimes very distasteful tasks that come our way; it is not the task itself, it is the way we do it that matters, and in there lies our strength, our ability to fulfil the Will of God and our ability also to hold that invisible key to the Mysteries which God never denies to the student who is worth while.

The experiences of the Egyptian neophyte take us far into that space which we call the invisible world. During the hours of sleep, all light and joy were experienced by him; when he returned he found the joy of the cup, and the lotus bowl, and the beaker from which he drank the blessed and sacred water. We search for that; perhaps we have not the privilege that we had in the past, when we were trained in those self-same things – memories, visions. But we can withdraw into the silence – even in this world of noise and tumult – and find God. And find God in a way that in the past – as neophytes in the Temple of Osiris – we did not, only our understanding, our ability to fulfil the cleansing and the purification of the body within and without; the cleansing and purification of the mind to make it strong enough to withstand the suggestions of the evil one; the cleansing of the feet before the next step; the cleansing of the heart by the gift of grace accorded to those who are humble of heart and can kneel before the altar; and the complete conquering of tasks of material life so that men may realise that in the material world we have a place as great as those who do not accept the things of the spirit, or bow the knees in praise and thanksgiving to the Father-Mother God, the God of Osiris, the God of Isis, the God of Jacob, the God of Moses, the God of Israel.

CHAPTER FOURTEEN

The Experience of Death and Resurrection

And so we return in thought to those moments when the child was dedicated in infancy by his parents for the service of the priesthood and is brought again to the temple to begin his training at ten years' old, and some special children at seven years' old. We have seen these children introduced to the small white cell in which they were to pass their days; and now we are touching them in thought as older children from seventeen to twenty years, taking the initiation which gives them the first benediction of the highpriest.

The cell is still white; it is narrower, very much smaller. The silence in it is deeper, because the student has given himself to the silence and within this cell he must study all physical and androgynous sciences; all sciences connected with the mineral world and the earth, the science of the beasts and the birds and the fishes, the science of the trees and the living growth from the soil; he must know the feel of the waking seed in his hand when the breath of God ruffles the corn fields before the reaping; he must submit himself to his masters and teachers in complete obedience; he must study the hieroglyphs deeply, for they are the symbols which lead man to an understanding of the Law of God. And above all must he study meditation – not as so many students study meditation today – but deeply, thoroughly, from the soul, until truth, the inner truth of God, has become an integral part of his being, which holds him with strength and purity till he is all truth.

Men say today, 'I live a true life, I do not lie or steal, I do not torture, or kill and, therefore am I a good man' – but you cannot be an initiate of the temple until you have gone down into the depths and searched your soul and made the truth which God has given you, the whole of your body, soul and spirit.

And at this moment the student in the temple would feel that his Masters were unsympathetic and aloof, he would see very little of them, they were apart from him for he must learn to tread the path of development alone, guided by them, able to pick up their guidance in the silence but not mixing with them, or becoming one with them in social life or amusement. But a child of God, dedicated to the Service of God through service to the temple, and his motto, the motto of the student in development, the same yesterday, today, and for ever, can only be read one way – wait and work.

Then there would come a day when the Masters of the temple would visit the cell of the student and the hierophant would come to him and say, 'My son, it is now time' – or my daughter 'it is now time for you to seek further a dedication to your Father-Mother God; you must go down through the gates of death and feel and know the meaning of death and the purpose of death, before you can touch the resurrection which leads you to the life of the spirit.'

The student would smile and go; he would follow humbly, with bowed head, in his simple grey garment, those who led him down those subterranean steps into the Hall of Initiation – and standing on end, at one end of the hall was a sarcophagus; he would look at this sarcophagus; he would look at the hierophant who led him by the hand, and his heart would begin to beat, and it is possible that fear would enter his thought for a moment. But the clasp of the hierophant's hand would give him power and confidence. With strong, slow steps he would walk forward silently beside him.

There would be three priests with him, and to one fell the duty of the explanation – 'Enter, my son, the sarcophagus is prepared for you, you must remain alone here until the death of man within you has taken place and you are ready to rise towards the Light of God'. Slowly, and with a still more quickly-beating heart, the student entered the sarcophagus; and it was closed and he felt more alone than he had ever felt in his cell. He tried to withdraw from his fears and from the darkness which surrounded him and to meditate upon the Love of God and the great mission he hoped to fulfil as a Priest of Isis, but he could do nothing. Time seemed not to exist; he was alone, completely and wholly alone; he could see now why his masters and teachers had been aloof, for that aloofness had prepared him for this much more dense and impenetrable loneliness. Then it would seem he slept.

The fluid part of the etheric body would be withdrawn; he would be conscious of an experience which perhaps he had not yet dwelt sufficiently in thought upon; the experience of the separation of the soul from the body and the severing of the cord; the cord was not really severed – the student was still alive in the body but the feeling was there and every sensation of dying must be experienced by the student, before the fulfilment of glory, which could only come if he could hold on without fear and accept the death of the body. That slow gradual separation which drew the soul spirit through the body of flesh, so that he felt light, conscious of light, conscious of colour, conscious of radiance in the darkness, which comes always at the moment of the severing of the cord.

You who deal with many who pass to the world of spirit in fear, know so well how a soul feels that severance of the cord, like a physical blow and then quiet, a long quiet and peace, almost as if the dove of peace descending upon him with its wings soaring above him gave him courage to rise above the material things of the earth – the glory of the life of the spirit. A long, long silence and then, as if the dream were still continuing, a beautiful figure appeared to him, a radiant figure of a woman clothed in all the glory of spirit robes, the radiance of the soul shining through the body, lightening the robes that they were as samite, mystic, wonderful. 'Who art thou who cometh to me in this moment of desolation?'. 'Oh! child of the light, I am thy spirit-sister, son of God – because thou hast shown courage of the severance of the cord, because thou hast held to the truth at the moment of death, I am permitted to be with you and to hand thee this bud. When

96

the bud blossoms they will come to release thee'.

She places her hand upon his shoulders and the power and the glory of the light which she brings flows into his body and he knows the ecstasy and the purity of true spiritual vision, to which he has remained in solitude so long; he has never touched the ecstasy of truth pulsing through his veins, filling his heart, giving his own eyes the Glory of God to shine through the density of the sarcophagus to the waiting priest.

'Do not leave me – wait beside me' – 'I may not, I have given thee the bud and when it blossoms they will come'. And he is again alone – no longer with the sweat of death and suffering upon his brow, only the great glory of the light of truth and of achievement in the service of God. A long silence and then the door of the sarcophagus is opened and the hierophant and the three priests stand there – 'Come, my son, thou has fulfilled the tasks set before thee, thou knowest the pain of death and the glory of resurrection." The body is stiff from lack of movement, as the student steps forth from the sarcophagus, two priests come forward to support him by the arms that he may not fall. In his right hand the bud is opening and he sees and smells the perfume of a perfect white rose, the only reward which he had, except the memory of the glorious beauty of the dream through which he had passed.

CHAPTER FIFTEEN

The Craftsmanship of the Children of the Nile

The land of Egypt was composed of soil and sand and gravel brought down from the great mountains which are now called the Mountains of Abyssinia and cast where the Nile should wash over them and cleanse them. The Nile itself had the blessing of that land, and a great and mighty and beautiful land it became. But at that time it was known as Khemu and lay under the hot sun parched, dry, except for the waters of the Nile.

Was it wonderful that those simple people of the valley, who came to inhabit the land of Khemu should make a god of that glorious river? It is difficult to understand that no man sought to penetrate to its source or seek the origin of its being? For all men believed that the Nile was indeed God, who prepared for their salvation the great floods which inundated the soil and gave them an opportunity to grow their rice and later their flax and corn. The corn came much later, but it plays a very important part in the history of Egypt, for it was the crowning of the Corn King and the Spring Queen which made one of the great temple rituals of the past.

The Nile divided the land. The Nile watered the land. The Nile made the land fertile by flooding with the rich mud from its bank the fields which the fellaheen prepared.

As we come from the world of Spirit and look down on the land of Egypt today, we see very little difference in the way the people live, from how they lived in those days. Some distant stirring of inherited memory made it possible for them to call to mind the plaited bench of the Valley of Atlantis, and in addition to the plaited bench, there was made from time to time a mat plaited of rushes culled in the valley itself from the swamps.

Egypt was rich in rushes. The banks of the Nile, from its source to its mouth, were encompassed, and still are in many places, with many varieties. Therefore, it was natural that these very simple people should draw rushes and of the rushes form mats which they gathered together in a rough fashion to form the little circular huts in which they lived.

The rush has many strange qualities, but two are pre-eminent. It is hollow, therefore any article made of it is light – light in weight. It is cool in summer and when it is laid, one thickness on another it is warm in winter, although there was never any cold there in that land as you know it here today.

When these early people had settled in the land for awhile, there came among them beings of another race whom they did not recognise. Instead of awkward, rather ungainly, bodies of the dark-skinned men who dwelt in these huts of plaited rush moving about rather like animals without any definite routine or purpose, there was noticed from time to time, a tall well-built sturdy man who was sometimes accompanied by a woman very much of the same build as himself, and these had red skins which you know as the skins of the ancient Egyptians. Their eyes were vivid blue, which was the colour of the Atlantean priesthood. The hair was black; it covered the head but it grew slowly and hung straight from a crown in the centre of the top of the head. They were a very placid type of people and were never hurried nor bothered like the first inhabitants of the land. They did not spread into the interior of the country at all; they remained close to the Nile, cherishing the river, loving its smooth clear waters, glorying in its mirrored beauty and remaining at all times close beside it.

They, too, plucked rushes and wove them, but it was not so rough as the early settlers. They made of these rushes baskets and cradles, such as Moses was laid within, and they placed their cradles in which lay their little ones in the shelter of the rushes, so that the bottom of the cradles floated gently upon the breast of the river itself.

In a sense they worshipped the Nile. But night and morning they gave praise to an unseen Being, whom they pictured above the clouds behind the blue sky basking in the light of the sun's rays, and they called him 'Ra'.

They were clever with their hands and desired to make symbols for the guidance of their fellows, therefore upon the sand they drew the symbol of Ra, the Sun-god, and when they tried to describe the way Ra crossed the sky from morning to nightfall, they added wings to the symbol in the sand, and thus the winged disc became the symbol of the first temple. You must distinguish between Horus the winged disc and Horus the Son of Isis and Osiris, for speech had not yet come to the children of the Nile; their only speech was in symbols. The woven rush gutter made in the sand for the water to run, formed designs and symbols and pictures were drawn in the sand itself with a sharpened rush. These were symbols through which the people spoke to each other.

Those first rude children of Egypt kept apart from these godlike beings. They muddled on in their strange little ways, living that odd life, very simple, needing very little food and practically no comfort or companionship.

But the children of the Nile were different. They grew in stature and in beauty and came very close to God. As craftsmen, there came a moment when they found the Nile mud as clay in their hands, and now, instead of drawing their symbols in the sand they made them in clay and placed them in the sun to dry. They were always improving upon these earthen vessels. They had no potter's wheel but became expert in rolling the clay round their closed fist or, to make a longer vessel, round the arm.

They would prepare little cages of reeds on which they plastered the clay, holding the vessel after it had been shaped in the sun to dry and while the simple children of Egypt made little progress, the children of the Nile developed many skills, and gradually developed their culture and knowledge.

They did not interfere with the first settlers at all, until the need came for them to build a temple and their desire was to capture the rays of the Sun in the temple, so that when he

100

disappeared at night he would leave his glory in the temple itself and not depart from them during the hours of sleep. So they pressed abroad, searching for materials of which they could build their temple. The first great temple which was completed by them was the Temple of Edfu and on this foundation the later Temple of Edfu was built. We are touching a period roughly a hundred years after the Temple of the South had been completed.

They found stone and they divided these stones into three types – one which was grapholite, one diorite, and the third and the hardest, granite. And they knew that the foundations of their temple must be builded of the hardest of the three stones, which was the granite, and composed of millions of grains of sand pressed into rock forms over aeons of time. It had to be hewed from the mountains and carried great distances. And although the children of the Nile could draw to their service the powers of the deva kingdom to lift these great weights of stone, they still needed workers who could bear the stone for them and whom they would surround with the power of the ether to enable the weight of stone to be carried. They did not undertake the work of that nature themselves.

A long time ensued when very little was done. Plans for the temple were drawn out in the sand. They were prepared on clay tablets with the aid of a pointed rush, which was filled with clay and hardened in the sand so that it became as solid as one of the lead pencils today.

Certain of their number were engaged in the preparation of the foundations of the temple and others, who could understand the symbols which the first settlers used, went abroad and mixed with the settlers, aiding them in many ways, adjusting their strange little rush mat houses, showing them how they could dig canals, to draw water to their doors and how they could make bridges over those canals, of hardened clay, which they could cross.

All these things and many more did the children of the Nile, for the first settlers in the land of Egypt. Thus a friendship grew up between them, and when the children of the Nile withdrew from the settlers, they were sad and alone. Some of the more venturous spirits among them made the long journey

101

that they might communicate with their guides· and counsellors and learn of them their ways and their customs.

When they came to these places by the river bank where the drawings were being prepared and they saw these gracious leaders with their tablets on which the designs had been made for the building, they were astonished and fell down and worshipped them, believing them to be gods come to earth.

Thus they came to offer their service to the great counsellors and master builders. The counsellors were gentle with them. They understood these simple people. Gradually, little by little, the great blocks of stone were brought from the mountains and hewn and beaten into shape for the foundations of the Temple of God.

Above them in the sky, Horus looked down upon them and shed his rays, and in the centre of the floor of the temple was prepared the great symbol of the Winged Disc, and the diorite stone was beaten with rock into many little chippings, and while the clay was soft to the touch the wings were filled with the chippings, so that the light of the Sun pouring down upon it, lit it, and made it into a symbol of holiness.

The king who eventually came to the Temple of Edfu held fast to the Winged Disc of Horus, and he was the first to bring into the temple service the workers in metal. So great was the service which was later given by these workers in metal that the king took no step without them. Their tools were stones and flints sharpened, their skill was the skill of the artist, and before he passed into his pyramid tomb he divided the workers in metal into two classes, the workers in base metal and the workers in precious metal. He called them both workers in metal in the service of the temple, and he called the one 'Worker in precious metal in the service of the temple' and the other he called 'Worker in base metal in the service of the temple.'

CHAPTER SIXTEEN

The Children of the Breath and the Child of the Life-Spark

When you read a book on ancient Egypt, especially on that period which touches the new and the old Stone Ages of Egypt, you will come across many phrases which show how little the historian of our day knows about those periods of the ancient past. Much of the detail of that time cannot be proved by the finding of stone tablets, or searching into ancient records.

One of the points that mystifies the archaeologist is on the question of clothes; another point is that of death.

This is because there were two distinct peoples in the land of Egypt – those who evolved from the life-spark of whom most of the Arabs of today are descended, and those who returned from Atlantis, the Children of the Breath incarnate by the Will of God for a special purpose – the artists, the makers of music, and the craftsmen.

The children of the life-spark became servants to the Children of the Breath. They could not create; they had no culture and therefore, they were called upon to use their physical bodies for physical labour. They did not desire to think for themselves, and were content to do the bidding of the Children of the Breath, and although some of these primitive people learned creative art from the Children of the Breath, they were few in number and widely separated throughout the land.

The Children of the Breath wore, first of all, the main rough

103

coats of skin reaching to the knees. Later they wore linen tunics, also reaching to the knee. The women wore long robes made first from a fabric prepared from the bark of trees, and since there were no trees in Egypt this bark was brought from the Sudan, which was a district of much wider extent than it is today, fertile and rich. During the period when the women's garments were prepared from a fabric of tree bark, the men wore skin, and later the women were able to weave thread and prepare linen and to make a white garment for themselves. The men wore tunics of the same material.

The hairdressing of the women varied. Some of them wore it loose, others wore it attached by a cord and others twisted their hair into a kind of handle on top of the head. Later, men and women alike wore the hair cut straight across the forehead and straight in the nape of the neck.

Both the men and women were skilled craftsmen. They could mould beautiful pots without the aid of a potter's wheel and polish these without the aid of a polishing stone.

In the sand they would find beautiful coloured stones and these they shaped into symbolic forms in which the bird played a large part, and polishing them, strung them on cords for their neck and wrist.

The archaeologist is also much puzzled by the beauty of craftsmanship of these ornaments, for they believe them to have been made by men who were only able to hew and carry rough stone. They do not know of the two distinct peoples.

The women of the life-spark who served the children of the Breath looked very much alike; therefore, they had painted on their arms, and later on their faces, symbolic pictures such as were used for stone ornaments, in order that they might recognise each other and, in a sense, belong to the child, or children of the Breath to whom they owed allegiance.

There was no question of payment for service at that time. The life-spark child was fed; he was given a plot of land where he could make his little hut, and he was cared for by the children of the Breath, who taught him such craft as he was able to assimilate.

When a great building, or temple was to be erected each family of the children of the Breath would lend so many servants and it was at these moments that confusion might have occurred. Therefore, the servants gave themselves willingly to having the symbol of their lord tattooed upon the skin, the body or the face. For this was a protection and no one would dare to harm such a one wearing a symbol and the one to whom that servant owed allegiance would see that he was not hurt, or injured in any way.

The workers in stone and the potters and those who prepared the plaited craft from reed, had been fulfilling their purpose for a very long time before the worker in metal appeared. For there was no metal at this time. The metal, largely copper, a little tin and a certain amount of iron, was brought from the Sudan on the backs of donkeys. Sometimes, when the donkeys were scarce, for they originally came from the Sudan, groups of men would carry large bales on their shoulders, walking or trotting for many miles.

The people of the Sudan differed from either of the races of Egypt. They were of immense strength – tall, well-built, with woolly, fuzzy hair and very little speech. They had little brain-power, and were primitive in their habits, only able to go, or to move where they were directed.

It is probable that the metal which was used at this time in Egypt came from Tanganyika, and we can visualise when the first bales of metal were brought to the children of the Breath they were puzzled as to what they could do with it.

Much of their work was carried out with stone arrow heads and rough tools shaped like chisels and hammers, not suited to work upon metal. They therefore sent out a call that someone might be sent to them who would be able to handle this strange substance. One day a caravan of merchants appeared from a different direction from the usual way from the Sudan, and a man who led the caravan became excited when he saw the metal. He was himself a metal worker and knew its value and he prepared tools with which he could work the metal. He was happy among the children of the Breath. He admired their craftsmanship, much of which was unusual in his eyes, and he remained with them, teaching them how to work the metal and showing them the uses to which it could be put.

So metal appeared for the first time in use in Egypt. Among the bales which came from the Sudan were wonderful elephant tusks; archaeologists examining their wonderful ivory statues are unable to understand how the Egyptians came by it. In fact, it was used only as ballast to balance the packages and the parcels and the bundles which were carried by the men and the donkeys.

Being hollow, precious material which could be harmed by exposure to the weather would be stuffed into the tusks, and they hung one on each side of the donkey, great white semi-circles in the sunlight.

The metal craftsman could also handle ivory, and the craft grew and became wonderful in the land of Egypt, for this man taught others and had many apt pupils to whom he passed the knowledge of the art of ivory carving.

A time came when precious metals arrived from the Sudan – gold and silver which were carved and prepared as symbols for the women to wear, and these were used with greater joy than the stones for which they searched in the sand. It was a joyous time in Egypt and a time of much prosperity.

Archaeologists are also puzzled by the different forms of the acceptance of death. The children of the Breath believed in rebirth, but they did not accept reincarnation in the flesh. They knew that when man was ready to leave the temple of the physical body, he went forward into another body in which he dwelt awhile and then into another body. They did not accept the fact that there was reincarnation in the flesh. They took great care of the body after death, these children of the Breath. They wrapped it in mats prepared from plaited reads and they blessed the body and they placed it under benches, the little tent-like places, waiting for the spirit to be wafted, as formerly, to the heights above the tableland.

But the children of the life-spark had no knowledge of these things. If they thought about them at all they knew that there would come a moment when something would happen to them, which would prevent them from living and working and that then their body would be left in the desert sand, to be covered by the wind which blew the sand over them, or to be cleared by the vultures. For the vulture was an important bird

106

in Egypt. You will find it used in many different symbols, and according to the direction in which the vulture is turned – so it holds a different meaning.

These discrepances puzzle the archaeologist because he cannot see why the body of one man should be wrapped and cared for, while the body of another should be left to be destroyed by carrion. But it was so, and just as an animal in the jungle today creeps away into its hole to die and no one troubles about the body, so the body of the child of the life-spark was disposed of by natural means.

There was no inter-marriage between the children of the life-spark and the messengers who brought the freight from the Sudan, although some archaeologists believe that the Sudanese later inter-married with the Egyptians and that a new race was born. This was not so. They had no desire to mix the one with the other. For their beliefs and ways of life differed from each other.

As the number of craftsmen in metal grew, visitors came from far countries to see the work which was done, and although there was no system of payment, there was a system of barter, and precious things were brought from India and Persia and China which were used by the children of the Breath in Egypt, so that when their temple was erected it was rapidly furnished with great luxury. They would exchange their metal goods, their ivory carvings, their pots, their ornaments with merchants who came from the distant lands of the East, and thus it was that much craft was introduced into Egypt and used in the temple which was not indigenous to Egypt.

Amongst the precious things which were brought from Abyssinia was a strange metal substance, a metal-like surface upon a stone back. Like a piece of rock split in half in which the halves that were formerly joined reflected like a mirror, and this the Egyptians readily accepted. At first it arrived in very small quantities, and the women would use a small piece of it to gaze at themselves and study their features. But later, when the people of Egypt found how valuable it was, large quantities of it were brought into Egypt.

From this strange stone were prepared the first mirrors

which were placed within the pillars of the great temples so that the lookers, who originally came from Atlantis, could read the future for the priests and the priesthealers in these glistening surfaces.

It was when these small pieces were first used by Egyptian women as you would use a small mirror that the women began to paint their eyebrows. They used a peculiar method of doing so. In the working of the copper the worker in precious metal would leave behind a very fine powder and this the women collected and mixed with clay. Their eyebrows were very prominent and very easily burned by the hot sun, and they began by putting this paste on the eyebrows as a protection for their eyes. It was cool and soothing in the heat of the sun. And then gradually they found different ways of using both the powder and the clay and they used it as an ornament.

So with the coming of the mirror came vanity and also the darkness which comes from the love of the world and worldliness, and these brought vanity and admiration of the personality, which are a snare and a danger for the children of the earth.

CHAPTER SEVENTEEN

Communication through Sound

When it became necessary to submerge a portion of the great valley which surrounded the tableland on which the great and glorious temple of the Father-Mother God stood, a large number of Masters were sent forth, a group to the north, a group to the south, a group to the east and a group to the west. That sending forth took place over a very long period of time. They were not just called and sent out as so many king's messengers into the void; they were prepared, and part of their preparation lay in linking with the first and second groups who had gone forth and who, studying earth conditions, prepared for the later Masters to follow them.

The children of the Breath came to the Nile valley. They arrived fully adult, descending through the ether and, wrapping around themselves according to the command of God the denser ethers as they made contact with them, so that when they awoke from the sleep of their coming, they were beings of flesh and blood clothed with the light of the Father-Mother God, breathed upon by His Breath, so that the Holy Spirit within them was of Him and with Him, beings of culture and wisdom, of spiritual understanding.

They came to earth for a special purpose, that they should separate from their twin souls in the etheric planes that these twin souls should be born anew, fully adult in the physical body after a sleep which to them was as the sleep of death is to you, leaving behind the place of light and entering into the flesh and the darkness of the earth plane.

But they came that they might fulfil their task of creation and bring into being children of the Breath, made of the flesh of their own bodies, blood of their blood, physical of their physical, completely, and yet ever of the Breath of God, holding within them the seed atom of the heart, the culture, the wisdom, the learning of the great Holy Temple. These children, fruit of the twin soul incarnate, came to earth as tiny, crying infants and grew under the tutelage of their parents to manhood and womanhood.

Thus you find a wonderful legend woven round Moses, who was a child of the Breath incarnate in the physical body, born into the physical world as a child. But he did not cry. He was joyous, full of joy; it was only when the various parents had spent continual time upon the earth plane that the sorrow of the earth plane entered into their souls and their children came to cry instead of to rejoice.

We have considered the great difference between the incarnate children of the life-spark and the incarnate children of the Breath, and we realise, therefore, how the land of Egypt came to be divided into two distinct portions; those with the spiritual culture and the wisdom of the place of light, endeavouring to build a foundation on the physical plane through all the denseness of material vibrations, and the children of the life-spark, their heads bent and grovelling in the dust, people who must achieve their culture and their spiritual knowledge through fulfilling their service to the children of the Breath in the physical plane.

The children of the Breath came into that fertile land surrounding the Nile valley. They looked always towards the symbol of Aquarius towards the Aquarian age, for which even in those far distant times preparations were being made. They increased in fairly large numbers and they began to feel that the time had come when they needed a leader. They communicated with their Father-Mother God and they asked Him that He would send them a king.

A long time elapsed before the Father-Mother God sent forth the second group of Atlantean Masters, a group that went to Egypt. There were two hundred and forty of these Masters; each one had held a specific and responsible place in the great Atlantean Temple; each one had his own work to do

110

upon the earth plane, and although all began in the Nile valley, all were not commanded to stay there, for one hundred and twenty remained in Egypt, the other one hundred and twenty being under the command of the Father in a different direction.

We have seen how these early children of the Breath prepared the drawings of their Temple, of the clay which they formed into tablets of the Nile mud. When they began to move away from each other and to use messengers for communication, they traced on tablets of dried mud, while the mud was wet, their messages. These were always symbolic – a large bird in flight, a small bird in flight, a stone pillar or a stone pyramid, a group of men carrying bundles on their heads, men kneeling, men attaching ropes to heavy stones, men cutting reeds and playing them, men cutting bigger reeds to make pipes. These symbols were the basis of the Egyptian hieroglyphs, and the one who went away to whom the messenger was sent, was thus kept in constant communication with his family, 'family' meaning the community, by messengers who were chosen from the life-spark because they could not read the symbols, carrying these tablets as you would send a letter from one to the other.

When the hundred and twenty special Masters came, they abode on the delta of the Nile. If they penetrated further up the Nile they did not remain very long. And here they prepared a very wonderful stone, a stone which was called diorite which could only be found in the delta of the Nile, very much like the quartz stones of Atlantis, transparent, malleable but unbreakable, and this was moulded by the children of the Breath who had already for some time dwelt in the Nile valley, into a shape upon which was inscribed in symbolic form the names of the Masters who came forth and who caused the stone to be prepared.

That stone still exists today in the city of Palermo and is known as the Palermo Stone. It bears the names of the hundred and twenty Masters into whose charge was given the land of Egypt by the Father-Mother God.

These Masters were called 'Bati', a word which the Egyptian translator describes as 'king' because king is the highest office he knows to describe it. A Bati is a Master to

111

whom we bow the knee, whom we face with humility, to whom we offer praise and thanksgiving, for he is chosen of the Father-Mother God for a special way of preparation. He is part priest, part angel, part minister and teacher and part king, and therefore you will realise how the children of the Breath reverenced their Bati, how they offered them homage and came to learn of them the culture which had continued in the great temple on the tableland long after these first children had come to earth.

At this time the study of sound began to increase. The child of the Breath in the Nile valley, standing by the flowing water in the early morning light, would breathe deeply, holding in the diaphragm and drawing in the Holy Breath, so that his body became still in the sight of God, and as he expelled at the end of his exercise he would utter the long, low 'A-a-a-h', and then he would call to his fellow across the river and he would draw the lips in for a moment, and 'O-o-o-h', and louder, 'O-o-o-h', and these sounds uttered in the silence of the great open spaces picked up the vibration of the ether around them. Here we find the child homesick probably for his great temple on the tableland, remembering the Alpha and the Omega, the beginning and the end. For a long time these two sounds were the only sounds uttered by the early children of the Breath.

Then came the 'E', your ordinary letter E, holding and dying away, the mother calling to her child, the child responding on the same note again picked up upon the ether. And then the 'I', the voice raised, watching the flight of the great Egyptian cranes, for the river cranes, which were symbolised in the writing over and over again until today, stand for one of the great Egyptian symbols.

And then the 'Oo-oo-oo', its intensity of sound in the centre, another call, another note, another sound.

Much later came a sound which is necessary for training the children of today which links with the zigzag of Aquarius, the sign of the Water, and again upon a deep breath the sound of the wind in the rushes, which precedes the storm in the ether, the sound which, dying away, traces upon the ethers of light the note of peace – 'Whe-e-e-e-w'. .Thus gradually more and more sounds were added and used in communication.

CHAPTER EIGHTEEN

Birth and Death amongst the two races in Egypt

We know from studying the history of Egypt that there came a time when a division was made between Lower and Upper Egypt. Upper Egypt was inhabited during those early days by the children of the life-spark, and Lower Egypt was inhabited by those great kings who came as highpriests and masters direct from Atlantis, reigning each for over one hundred years, masters also of the Atlantean temples.

The speech of the children of the life-spark was guttural sound with very little form or direction in it. They had not yet reached the stage of calling each other by names or appellations, and we realise that these simple people, descended as they were from the group soul and thus part of the animal creation, were evolving slowly into light, still in those ancient days holding many of the ways of the creature.

When an animal is about to give birth to young she creeps into a quiet place where she can remain undisturbed. Sometimes she finds that quiet place among friends, sometimes she even prefers to be alone, using her own instinct to know what is best for the young she is about to bring into the world.

These children of the life-spark held that way of life very strongly. When the mother-to-be drew near the time of birth she would cover herself with a long strip in the form of a garment of some soft texture woven from the grasses, provide herself with a pitcher of water and a few cakes baked in the

113

sun upon hot stones from rice and water mixture, and, thus equipped, she would go away into the desert until she felt sure that she was able to resume her normal life among her people again.

Exactly the same thing happened at the moment of death. The dog or the cat, feeling that the moment has come when it is of no further service to its friends and companions among men will, in the normal way, unless it is much overbred, creep away into a quiet place that it may be alone to die. This attribute the children of the life-spark also held. When they came to a point when they felt that their physical body was failing and there was no further good to be served by them remaining in the community, they would go into the desert to die. They did not voice it as 'death' for they had no knowledge of words, but they knew that when one of their number crept thus away they would not see him again. They did not trouble about him any more than the friends of the animal would trouble to go after him and find out what happened. Hence the desert in places was strewn with skeletons, which the white warm sand would cover as it was blown across the vast open space.

The children of the Breath were quite different. These were the children of Lower Egypt. They were perfect twin-souls, each cleaving to the other and having no purpose with any other member of the community, light and bright in the sight of God, enfolded in the power of the Holy Breath, concentrating their thoughts upon God and watching the flowing of the Nile down to the sea.

Each day they would set aside a period of time together, each pair, when they would move in their slow, careful fashion away from the community and find a quiet place where they would sit to speak to God, and in this speech with God they would learn of His will for them, not so much as individuals, but as a community, becoming even greater by the addition of more twin-souls, who, directed by the Father, came to earth to join them and to fulfil themselves in His service.

During these quiet periods they would concentrate upon the ether around them and draw from that ether light, which would help them to expand that inner light of the spirit which

114

they possessed and thus, looking at them from a distance as they sat in the desert, one would not see bodies at all but beings entirely of ether and light vibrating with sound, so closely were they encircled with the etheric light of the plane from which they had come.

During these quiet spells, with their consciousness raised to their own plane of consciousness, they would be instructed, each individually, on their fulfilment of their life span. If they had made mistakes in the preparation of the tablets, in their designs of birds, symbolic matters on the tablets themselves, they would be given the correction that they would make good when they returned to the community.

They would be given designs for their craftsmanship, inspiration of a very high order. Much of the work which was done with the rushes was indeed directed from a higher plane of consciousness than from the earth.

From time to time one would return from the delta, bringing with him one of these great stones of diorite, and each in turn, these twin-souls, would gaze upon the stone and read the will of the Father-Mother God mirrored in its facets.

So they dwelt much in the ether. In the early morning before sunrise and towards the going down of the sun you would see these pairs of people making their way to their own quiet spot and resting in the light of the Father-Mother God.

Gradually they came to take responsibility for the community and to draw into that community the children of the life-spark from the far desert.

There was a great difference between the masters among the children of the Breath and the masters of the life-spark. For gradually, as there rose among the children of the life-spark those who were physically and mentally stronger than the majority, they gained the power of leadership. They were hard taskmasters, commanding and demanding immediate obedience no matter how difficult the task, unrelenting towards the one who failed, and demanding such severity of labour that the unfortunate children could hardly achieve their will.

It was these who first used the rod to beat the bodies of their servants. It was these who devised the tortures which could hurt the physical body and sometimes make the physical body useless through torture and suffering. Therefore under that yoke the children of the life-spark groaned much and eventually they came towards the children of the Breath to offer to serve them.

They came with much humility. They had very little skill and very little knowledge, and they treated the children of the Breath as gods – so tall and straight were they, so clear their eyes, so radiant their looks, so pleasant and gentle their ways, that these poor souls fell before them and offered them worship and praise.

The children of the Breath showed the children of the life-spark many ways in craft and preparation, and under their guidance they became skilled; their strength in the happy atmosphere increased and the children of the Breath were well rewarded for their work.

But they were conscious of certain differences, especially at the moment of life and death, between themselves and between the children of the life-spark, and therefore, there was a barrier which could not be crossed. The two were apart and together. The children of the Breath in these moments of silence gained much in the radiance of light which the Father-Mother God poured out upon them, and they were glad that they could pass some of that light to the children of the life-spark, that they might feel the warmth of it and respond with gladness.

There were no rulers until the coming of the Bati, and these hardly ruled. They were companions, they were highpriests of the temple, as the children of the Breath had known them in Atlantis. Therefore, the community of the children of the Breath was one of equality, except that as time passed there came upon them a great distaste for the ways of earth, and though the young were radiant and strong and ready to take up life on earth, and to go forward with it, their parents and grandparents began to be weary of earth and to seek a quiet place of meditation more often, until there would appear times when the spirit was hardly within the physical body – it was away, even from the child of the Breath.

When the children of the Breath withdrew together to praise

God, they would use the power of the breath to manifest sound. Drawing in the diaphragm, deeply and slowly they would draw up the breath from the pit of the stomach on the sound of 'o' (au), and when the breath was exhaled they added the sound of the closed lips, which is 'om' (aum), so that the intaking and the outgoing of the breath became 'om' (Aum).

As their time upon the earth plane became more weary they would retreat into the silence to increase the power of 'Om', and thus they communed with the place of light and found the physical body, which encased by then only the personality with occasional visits of the soul, a weariness and a trouble to them. They remembered that once on a time they had watched highpriests and priests going down the side of the mountain from the temple on the tableland to fetch souls who were ready to leave the valley, and they remembered that these souls were to be found upon benches and later in little huts of plaited boughs and grasses and leaves. So they prepared, or had prepared for them the mastaba, the little narrow hut of plaited reeds in which they could shelter and find peace, for they knew that there would come one day when they would not return, and those who belonged to their community would let time elapse and finally follow, until they found the mastaba and within it the body, which had housed the soul, which had finished with earth and gone to join the highpriests of the temple in the place of light.

Then there came into being a ceremony. They would take down the mastaba and, using the soft covering of plaited reeds, wrap the body in it and bring it back to their place of meeting.

Thus we come to the great difference between the two peoples, for the children of the Breath never touched the body. The body was borne and prepared by those children of the life-spark who, working for the children of the Breath were in sympathy and understanding with their ways and gave them reverence, and therefore used with reverence the spice and precious herbs, in preparing the body for the burial.

The burial was not in the earth, or in the pit dug down in the soil. A stone cavern would be prepared beneath the sand and a flight of steps down into that stone cavern would enable

117

the body to be carried within it. But those who believe in reincarnation and are interested to know the place that the soul held in ancient Egypt will remember that the chambers of the embalmers in the later great temples were always manned by the descendants of the children of the life-spark, never by the children of the Breath, for the children of the Breath had interest only in the soul-spirit, which having left its human habitation was no longer with them.

If you observe pictures of ancient Egyptian temples you will find some of the early ones very simple, almost like caves, but in all you would find on one side of the entrance the mastaba, no longer of plaited rush, but a stone bench where the child of the Breath went when he knew that the etheric around him could hold him in the physical body only a little longer.

On that bench he waited in the shadow of the temple of Holiness for those of the world of spirit to fetch him. There his body would be found, as a rule, in the morning light.

These children of the Breath, even long before they had their own temple, were understanding and practiced extreme discipline upon themselves through meditation and concentration. Only thus could they escape what was for them a world of drudgery into the place of light where they knew God.

Therefore, the etheric light within them shone, shone from within to without till they were filled with radiance, until that moment when the soul, although perhaps still joined by the silver cord to the physical body, was ready to return to worship God in its own place.

CHAPTER NINETEEN

The Work of Amen Emaht

(Also known as Amenemhet I. 12th Dynasty 2000-1970 B.C.)

Oneferu – Ninth Divine Master of the Temple of Atlantis – incarnated at On as highpriest healer in the temple which later became known as the Temple of Isis at Heliopolis, and when the Master Oneferu first took over the charge of the temple it was but a very small part of the life of the nation.

It was a place apart where men could find sanctuary and peace. It was a training school for the young priests, who sought to educate themselves in the precincts of the temple for the duties of ministering to the altar of the Most High God.

It was a training place also for those groups of young girls, who were prepared through the study of the ritual of the temple, to undertake the specially appointed dancing, those wonderful rhythmic movements of the body which constituted the Egyptian dances.

Further, it was a training place for the musicians who gave their services to the temple, and it was a place where those among the peoples of that great land who wished to educate a child, or children in the service of God, in the service of the temple, could bring them for preparation on that first stage by the priest.

They could take the child, who in his tender youth could not learn much at the hands of the priest, home with them and train him according to the command of the priest for his important service later. Above all, it was a sanctuary set apart for the worship of God, where the High Angels and the

Seraphim and the wondrous Beings surrounding the Father-Mother God came from time to time, to accept the worship of the multitude and pour out upon them the power and the glory and the majesty of God Himself.

The highpriest would direct the whole organisation of the temple; through him would be poured the rays used by each leader of each group of students, the rays used by the healers, and the rays of glory which prepared the Holy of Holies in the name of the Most High God.

While Oneferu was still but a young man, deep in reverence and looking to all for godliness within the temple walls, there came to him one morning a young man, one of ancient lineage, of culture, whose education from his cradle had prepared him for a place of truth and trust. His face was round, as the faces of the ancient Egyptians were, the head well set upon the shoulders, the neck somewhat thicker than that of man today. The ears were well set back on the head, the eyes piercing, deep clear blue, the skin ruddy, almost brown as if it had been coloured by much sunshine, but so was the skin of the ancient Egyptian. His hair was coarse; straight, jet-black, cut close to the head in the front where it fell on the forehead as a frame and straight from the lobe of the ear round the back of the neck to the other ear again.

He wore the white tunic of the youth of a great household, a tunic which was looped upon the shoulders by the Zodiacal sign of his birth and his Sun sign upon the left engraved in silver, which was a rare and precious metal, and round the brow a band of coloured linen in the centre of which, over the third eye, was fixed a stone.

The stone showed the priest Oneferu the descent of this young man from the moment that his great grandfather had left the side of the Father-Mother God to come to earth. The name of the young man was Amen Emaht, Amen being the name of the temple in which his forbears had served, and Emaht his family name, a name by which he would be called by his family and his fellows.

He came barefoot; he knelt before the highpriest and offered him service. The highpriest called for the oils of the anointment and he anointed the young man with the oils

120

required for the service of kings, for in a very short time this young man became King of Egypt.

We hear of him in history as Amen Ra, and by other names which have almost the same meaning; but it is good that we should remember this one by the name by which he was known so many thousand years ago in the temple.

It was at this moment that the separation of the physical from the spiritual worlds became a thing of completeness. Until then the Hierarchy of Heaven had descended by the command of the Father-Mother God from time to time to enter the temple and to leave power and their benediction there.

But the time was coming when man's descent into matter must be deeper than it had ever been before, and if the Hierarchy bring into the precincts of the temple the glory and the power direct from God, the hardening of the acceptance of the way of life in the physical world cannot be as complete physically as our Father-Mother God would have it. Therefore, it is at this moment that we contemplate the withdrawal of the spiritual Hierarchy so that their power could only be accepted by the ministering highpriest healer and given forth by him where he was called upon to give it.

We are preparing for the coming of the Spiritual Hierarchy into earth again. We must therefore approach their coming with a certain measure of understanding by awakening the ancient memory of the great void left in the temple when they withdrew.

That occurred in the Temple of On which later became the Temple of Isis under the guardianship of the Master-Initiate Oneferu, and with the acceptance of Amen Emaht the First, for there were other Amen Emahts. But it is Amen Emaht the First who was the great one, much blessed by the Father-Mother God.

He was a great builder. He caused stones to be brought from distant lands and additions to be made to the temple. He stood upon the desert sands and gazed afar into the distance, that he might receive the inspiration necessary for his architects, masons and workers.

He it was who instituted that little order of men who,

121

though outside the temple and not considered priests or healers, nevertheless gave great service to the temple as architects and craftsmen. He it was who called these men 'craftsmen' where today they are called 'masons'. They grouped themselves in an order ordained by the highpriest, and a special portion in the centre of the great temple was set aside for them.

This was known and recognised by a carpet of special paving stones in squares of black and white, and it looked like a great black and white chequered carpet. At the four corners were tassels also prepared in the stone, tassels which signified the symbol of the order of men, who entering the temple, not trained or ordained as highpriests, not come after the order of Melchizadech, but men who gave their lives to the service of the temple, that the materialisation of all that concerned the spiritual temple should be in hands which knew the value of worship and praise, of humility and grace.

Amen Emaht prepared also a court within the great palace, the structure of which had already been builded before he took charge of it. Within this palace he called large groups of nobles, and here again he also brought the first touch of materialism into the palace which had been governed entirely by the priests. Now it became a thing of the people, and the nobles whom he called from his lands afar and sent to come and serve him were called upon to give dues in money, not only for the support of the palace but also for the support and extension of the temple. This was the first time that any child of the Breath had been called upon to contribute material means to the upkeep of the temple.

Amen Emaht would admit only those nobles who were prepared to give their dues, for among the nobles of the land of Egypt were many who took all they could, accepted all they could at the hand of the Father-Mother God and gave Him nothing, not even praise or worship. Amen Emaht determined that all this should be finished with, that every man who accepted the privileges of the court should contribute of his revenue, which was immense, to the holding up of the court, and that every man who was called upon to serve the court should also serve the temple and prepare his dues for the temple

122

in the temple service. It was largely from these nobles there descended that band of craftsmen which are now designated masons.

So we see the court and the temple no longer separate but together, and as the work of the court encroached upon the work of the temple it helped the temple to come more and more into material conditions and to become one with the court.

The last matter that Amen Emaht demanded from the highpriest before he completed his work in the joining of these two great forces, was in bringing the dancing girls to the court that they might demonstrate the movements of the ritual of the temple, which was the ritual of the Hierarchy of the Father-Mother God.

Amen Emaht was a great builder. A Master craftsman, a man of great beauty of countenance and feature, a man of great knowledge, wise in the law of the world, wise with the wisdom of the temple. We see him joining the wisdom of the court, with the wisdom of the temple.

We see him teaching his people that man was on earth not by accident, but in order that he should fulfil the one place that man meant for him, and that to fill that place he must contribute to the structure that supported him, not only through his wordly means, but through his worship, his praise and his humility.

CHAPTER TWENTY

The Temple of On

There is a certain symbolism which is known to those who study today the Inner Mysteries but which cannot be read by those who are not versed in such learning. We need to understand the inner meaning and obtain insight into these great Beings of the past who were commanded by our Father-Mother God to take charge of certain work for Him in service to humanity. Yet although we hear today of great humanitarian works being undertaken, we must not forget that they were undertaken under different auspices and in different surroundings in that distant past.

There was a radiance in the land of Egypt which emanated from the City of On. Today, it would be pronounced Ŏn, but those who trod the desert of the past called it Ōn. We pronounce it with a ring, or rhythm, because it is a word of very great importance, linking closely with the still greater world of power which is used on certain occasions by Egyptian guides and teachers, that wonderful word Om.

Later on, when greater things came to make themselves felt in the culture of Egypt, and men's minds were directed towards intellectual pursuits, the town of On was renamed and was called Heliopolis.

Greek intellectual thought was beginning to be introduced into Egyptian educated or cultured circles; and here we are touching something of importance, for Atlantean culture had a very great part to play in Greece and many things were taken to

124

Greece from Atlantis. The simple language spoken by those whom you would call peasants or rebels in Greece today, is not only of Atlantean origin but has many Atlantean sounds and syllables in its composition. Therefore, we see the merging of two important waves of Atlantean culture. Although the word aristocrat is used today to describe one of noble or kingly blood and descent, we can also use the word aristocrat in describing those mighty teachers who came from Atlantis and who merged their learning with the learning of the cultured peoples, with whom they mixed.

The Temple of Heliopolis is important in our lives today because we must relive those ancient cycles of the past. There was much that happened in that city and in and around those temples which is being worked out in the life of civilised man today. So important was this cultural centre that there was one directed to it from the planes of light, one Oneferu, Ninth Master-Initiate of Atlantis, and he came into full incarnation of the physical body to guide and direct the temples of On, for there were several, and in incarnation with him also was his twin and female soul, Oneferua. Oneferu was the chief Master-Initiate of the great Temple of On, and therefore he had very much to do with the guidance of the people of that day, and he would quite naturally guide the children of light in the temple today, for today the work of Oneferu and Oneferua lies in building anew the Temple of Light in preparation for the Christ of the Aquarian Age.

Oneferu had been Master-Initiate of the Central Temple of On for quite a considerable time when he felt that there was great need of a temple of healing, that the small chamber which was set apart for healing was insufficient and was also insufficient for the glory of such a great and wonderful temple. Therefore he caused to be built a very glorious temple of healing. The glistening white stone, the valuable coloured marbles, the gold for the ornamentation of the pinnacles were brought from far eastern countries, and day by day ships came up the silver Nile bringing their precious burdens to the quayside of the temple, for the temple of On was on a most precious and beautiful portion of the Nile. From the roof of the temple, from the little square house in which dwelt the Oracle,

125

there could be watched day by day the silver stream of the Nile, wending its way towards the mighty ocean, and up and down the stream came the boats bringing their precious burdens, from far and near for the service of the temple.

It took a very long time for the Master-Initiate, Oneferu, to make up his mind where he would have this temple built. At one moment he desired it near the water, at another that possibly the Nile in flood might represent a danger to this glorious edifice which he planned, and so eventually it was built within sight of the Nile, a little distance from the main temple of On. When the first stones were laid, it was called the Fountain of the living Sun, the architects of that time knew that such a temple planned in the mind of their Master-Initiate would take a very long time to build. Therefore, they prepared rooms where they undertook drawings and plans, and other rooms for the preparation of the hangings and the rich silks which were brought from the East, and the valuable dyes which came from Palestine and various parts of Syria, were all assembled in great store-houses, which were erected before even the foundations of the temple were laid.

But Oneferu, who held much power with water, decided that in some way he must bring the waters of the Nile close within the shadow of this new temple. He therefore caused a square courtyard to be prepared and he ordered that in the plan of the temple the courtyard should be surrounded by the healing rooms, but that the centre portion of the courtyard should be prepared as a lake, and within this lake, by pipes and aqueducts, should approach the waters of the Nile. Three times a day pipes were opened which poured from three sources the water from the Nile into the basin, and it was arranged in such a way that as the water filled the basin, so was the soiled water ejected deep down into the soil, to return after purification to the Mother Nile herself.

In the centre of the lake Oneferu caused a great light to be placed upon a pinnacle, and his light revolved, and at all hours of the day and night the beams of the sun and the beams of this lamp were thrown out on to the distant desert, so that travellers who brought the sick to the door of the temple were guided by the rays of the light. Over the doorways to the courtyard were placed images of the sun and its rays, heavily made in beaten gold, and all who entered reverenced the sun and the light which was shed from the great lamp in the centre of the lake. This lamp directed the rays of power, and these rays of power were mirrored in the lake itself, until Oneferu, walking slowly at eventide round the great basin, did exclaim. 'Truly, our Father-Mother God is good, for He has guided to our portals the lamp of Truth, and He will send from far and wide teachers and healers who will minister to the people with the power of the Temple of the Living Sun.'

For many years Oneferu did prepare the temple for the reception of the sick, and he was visited there by many teachers and masters who came from afar, and who would have placed him apart in a small chamber that he might not touch those who came who were not worthy to touch the power of light within the precincts of the courtyard.

To Oneferua was given the work of guidance in the building and the preparation of the temple of healing, and she did greatly desire that colours should be used in these precious silk hangings, in order that special rays should be directed through them for the healing of the sick. Both had studied in the Temple of Asklepios and knew the value of dreams, and they called towards them many from the East who helped them to design the chambers of healing.

These chambers were built, each one of four walls, square and beautiful, alongside the great lake in the centre, and in the wall of each chamber was a small white marble vessel into which purified water, warm for the use of the patients, was always pouring. To each chamber was assigned the colour for the special disease to be treated there. Then came the question of the healing of the children, and in this Oneferua was firmness itself, for she would not have the children mingle with the adults; she would have them in a temple apart. Therefore, Oneferu called the architects and his designers and he did command them that they should listen to Oneferua and build for her and her work only a temple of healing for the children. This temple also was built beside the courtyard of the Fountain of the Living Sun, and at eventide Oneferua and Oneferu, when the day's work was done, would move gently beside the lake and contemplate the doings of the day. They would dwell apart while in the small circular temple at the south end of the lake, or they would concentrate on those many sick who had been unable to visit the temple for their treatment.

Within this sanctuary of peace there was light – light undefiled and unharmed, for the darkness had not touched the Temple of the Living Sun. The fountain in the centre glowed in the dusk, and the great Eastern moon shone above, casting its shadow into the pool. Those who worked within the temple came at the hour of ten to be blessed by Oneferu before they slept, and each came to bring his report of the day's work and of his patients, and to leave with Oneferu the names of those who had presented themselves for the first time. When a patient presented himself he was received by one of the lesser priests of the temple in the outer chamber beyond the courtyard, and there he gave the particulars required of him. Then, having been regaled with fruit and cold water drawn from a running pipe, he was placed upon a couch and left to relax. Following the relaxation he was dismissed and his name brought forward on the tablets, so that Oneferu should give his opinion of the disease and of the treatment to be used at the hands of Oneferua, and in all things, Oneferua, with her deep intuitive knowledge of the realms of light and her hearing of the voice of light, did draw from light the direction which governed the life of the temple. And Oneferu bowed the head and listened, for ever it is the female soul who hears the Word and the male soul who acts upon it.

Following the benediction of the night, all concerned in the temple service went their ways to the small chambers in which they slept, above the confines of the temple; chambers where openings to the sky were never closed, chambers where the power of God in the heavens and the planetary candles of light could be contemplated by all who served the temple. There they shed their garments of the day, resting awhile in the cool running water of the baths provided for the ablutions of the temple servants, until they went their way to their hard couches and slept until the sun rose. No sick people ever dwelt within the temple, they came only for their treatment and went away again.

128

When the sun rose in the morning, one whose duty it was as a warden, came forth and, standing upon the southern edge of the lake in the centre of the courtyard, he waited until the light of the sun gilded the great lamp. Then he struck upon a bell and that bell called all temple servants to their exercises. For a period of time, roughly half-an-hour, the silence of meditation dwelt upon the temple. None disobeyed, not because they dare not disobey, but because they had no wish to do so.

The ablutions of the servants in the temple were of great importance, for they bathed their bodies in cold running water before they donned the white robes of their service. These white robes were distinguished by girdles and badges from one another, so that a servant of the first year could never be mistaken for a servant of the third year. At each corner of the great lake, carved in the living marble, were four tassels, and these, to this day, have ever been used in the inner mysteries and in the decorations in the temple.

In the Temple of Light, Oneferu undertook one special work. He it was who, with his power of light and strength of purpose, could build in the etheric the exact counterpart of all that was created upon the earth. There were very few, even among the Master-Initiates, who could build an etheric counterpart, but Oneferu, the great architect, could do so. That is why today, in a world troubled and torn with disharmony, he has, at the command of his Father-Mother God, come to earth to build the Temple of Light in the hearts of men and its counterpart in the planes of light.

CHAPTER TWENTY ONE

The Halls of Records and of Preparation

The great healing temple which Oneferu caused to be constructed under his direction was a little distance from the temple of worship, connected with the city of On. There were two similar halls built as part of the healing temple.

The temple itself was in the centre, and on the right was a similar temple which held the records of the work of the building on one side, and the records of sickness, curative treatment and cures on the other. These two sets of records were under the same roof but on different sides of the hall. The hall on the other side of the temple of healing was one in which there were prepared the healing waters and the potions which were administered to those to whom they were prescribed. Both temples were of great interest to all who worked in connection with them.

Attached to the Temple of On was the Hall of Records. The walls were composed of glistening white quartz, the floors of a transparent stone of extreme beauty, green in colour, laid upon foundations of white marble, so that nothing should detract from the colour given out by the stone. This stone was extremely precious in Egypt; it had been brought from a great distance and was therefore costly to use. It could be bent only; no tool had ever been discovered to break it, nor could it be chiselled or cut in pieces. It was brought to the temple in square sections unchanged by nature for the use of her children of light.

130

Attached to the walls were tiers upon tiers of shelves, these shelves divided into sections, each holding its own records. The sections were numbered, and the colour of the stone used for the record was placed beside the number. The records were kept in glyphs, the meaning of the glyph varying according to the colour of the stone. Thus, if you take your word 'holy', 'holy', when it was represented by an amethyst stone would mean 'holy', but 'holy' represented by a blue, a green, a violet, or a jade stone, would mean something quite different. Therefore the recording of these glyphs was a work of intellectual attainment, and those who were engaged upon the work were men of learning and wisdom.

On the one side of the hall were the glyphs which recorded the building and the preparation of the temple, and on the other were the glyphs recording the patients who received treatment, and the results. Each patient's vibration was of a different colour; therefore the colour of the patient appeared beside his name upon the glyph. These colours were introduced by means of chiselled stone placed in small sockets on the outer edge of the covering of the glyph.

The other hall was of much greater importance to the healers even than the records. It was like a wonderful room of light. Shutters in the roof were drawn to admit the greatest possible amount of sunlight. In the centre was a white marble table, round in shape, and kept of polished cleanliness. On this table was a ledge, which today you would call a tray, and this was divided into twelve sections, each section bearing one of the signs of the Zodiac. Upon these sections were placed glasses of water, potentised by the power of special groups of healers and submitted to the rays of the sun, which potentised them still more strongly. Where the addition of another colour was required, the glass would be placed upon a tiny disc of coloured stone, so that the colour drawn through the water by the power of the stone should also add its ray to the power in the water.

These waters were never placed in closed vessels. They were covered with small discs which fitted them as covers and placed upon a shelf for when they were ready to be used by the patients. The sign of the Zodiac which was predominant in

131

the life of the patient, was also predominant in the healing action of the rays.

At one end of the temple were enormous slabs placed away from the wall, so that working healers could move on all sides of them, and here, under transparent covers, were placed the herbs and blossoms, brought from great distances, for the preparation of healing drinks. These herbs and flowers, when seen beneath these transparent covers, were as fresh as the day they were picked, and had you removed a tiny portion of the stalk, you would have been able to feel the moisture of the sap.

These blossoms and leaves were floated in glasses of specially prepared water, according to prescriptions given by the healer attendant on a certain number of patients. These glasses were then exposed upon another table to the full rays of the noonday sun only. Therefore, they were exposed for only a few moments of each day. On other marble slabs at the side of the room were other herbs and blossoms, which could be used for outward application only, and these were incorporated in precious oils and balsams brought from far distant countries, making those pastes and pomades which were used for the healing of wounds and of sores and ulcers.

There were in that time many cases of enlarged blood vessels and veins, and for these were used always a preparation of olive oil and sweet almond oil, not bitter almond oil, violet leaves cut into very small pieces, and other healing herbs, such as balsam and thyme. But these blossoms and herbs were not found in Egypt; they had to be brought from countries in which they were grown.

For small children, a special unguent was made of sweet almond oil, beaten to a paste, to which was added the petals of the precious crimson rose from the gardens of the Temple of the Little Yellow Flower, and that temple of healing links strongly with the work of Oneferu.

The workers in the central temple of healing wore white garments, with girdles and badges showing to which temple they were attached. Those who worked in the Temple of Records wore garments of dark blue, soft and silky in texture, with girdles of silver and silver bands with badges upon the shoulders.

The Master-Initiate in the temple of healing wore, in addition to his head covering, a band round the forehead containing a jewel which noted his number among the Initiates of Atlantis.

The Master of the Hall of Records wore a deep sapphire on his forehead, attached by a band round the head, but no headdress.

The workers in the Temple of Preparation wore garments exactly the same in shape, but of that peculiar blue-green which was the colour of the Temple of Isis, and on their heads small round caps, underneath which the hair was confined, and a wide band of silver round the brow, holding the stone which linked them with the Master-Initiate of the healing temple.

The legs were bare in all temples, and a form of sandal made of plaited grass was worn within the confines of the temple. Those who worked among the flowers and the herbs had no badges, but heavy girdles of white cord clasped by a single head of a snake with vivid ruby eyes.

If at any time mistakes were made in this temple which called for some form of discipline or punishment, the white cord was taken from the worker and a dark blue cord without a badge of any description was substituted. This was considered an ugly and shameful thing to happen. You will find many people who will wear a belt or girdle of any colour whatsoever so long as it is not a dark shade of blue; thus is their memory awakening to some work which they fulfilled in the Temple of On.

CHAPTER TWENTY TWO

The Ceremony of Sleep in the Temple of Isis

The training of the students in the Temple of Isis depended largely upon the greatest gift of God which was love, and the gift which was worth everything else, sleep, for through sleep the initiate and the priest link with the Divine Father-Mother.

We will call the Father-Mother 'Ptah', because it is as Ptah we knew Him when we served in the Temple; Ptah, as the Father-Mother God, created through Adam-Evam, Arbal-Arbel and later Arbel came to earth in the physical body of the Master Jesus. The twin-souls of Ptah were created always in groups of three and therefore Arbal-Arbel had two brothers who were also twin-souls, the first being Enos-Enoi and Osiris-Isis. These were the two groups, the Enos group and the Isis group who were destined to become the parents of all the Ray children, all the Children of the Breath.

If you think of one of your ordinary families on the earth and you go back a long, long time in thought, you say 'That is a very old family; it is descended from that wonderful Knight who came to our shores with William of Normandy'. You realise that the direct sons and daughters of William of Normandy would have borne much of the characteristics of their father, but that, as the descendants moved forward into the future and they inter-married with the children of other noble families and sometimes, perhaps, one would join himself with one who came from a less noble family, the blood became intermingled and the traits of the father no longer came through in the same way.

134

This would be marked particularly through the power we call 'love' which is light, so that the father, if he were linked directly, as he should be, with the Father-Mother God, would be able to make contact with the power of the spirit very much more easily than would the great great grandson.

Aeons of time have passed since Ptah created Enos-Enoi, and the children who were their descendants are now very much further from God than were Enos-Enoi themselves. They would, therefore, find it harder to make contact with the power of the Father-Mother himself.

So gradually through the ages we have watched the physical-material creeping in and overshadowing the spiritual until it becomes more and more difficult and causes greater strain and stress to the children of today, who want to make contact with the Father-Mother in all His beauty and to accept at His hands the power of His Love. For this is the greatest thing that God can give to man and the most wonderful and beautiful gift that man can accept from God.

Those early Initiates who came to earth and founded the Temple of Isis were Beings of light. They found it difficult to become accustomed to the body of flesh, and upon the body of flesh they must place yet other bodies which were garments of material, and these they made as simple as possible, after the fashion of the forming of the ectoplasm which covered all who came in their radiance to worship in the great Valley of Praise.

They found the physical body extremely burdensome and their one desire was to be able to fulfil their material duties in such a way that they might return to the plane of light from which they had come and spend a while far away from the physical body.

This again was all in the plan of the Father-Mother God because, if the soul had not desired to leave the physical body, the physical body would have borne so great a strain that the organs would have had no peace, no time for rest or refreshment. Therefore it was good that the great priesthood of the temple should desire to escape the physical body at given moments to dwell beside the Father-Mother God in the place of peace, and they called this escape 'sleep'.

Set periods were appointed for this sleep. They did not just

135

go to sleep when the sun set and wake with the rising of the sun. Their praise and their worship concerned the sun, for the emblem of their temple was Ra, the Sun god. But they needed much more time in the world of spirit than just those hours of darkness, and therefore periods were appointed, during which the main Temple itself was given up to the hours of sleep, in order that those who ruled and governed the temple should accept the love of God at His own Hands and bring it back to the physical body, holding and treasuring it until it was needed for the strengthening and the upbuilding of the souls of men.

For this, a ceremony was founded in the temple and the great ones, the Master-Initiates, were called to recline on couches, which surrounded the outside walls of the central temple. Veils, which were somewhat like the fishnets of today but woven in the colours of the rays used in the temple, were let down from the roof of the temple to the floor, so that although the reclining figures were partly visible to the assembled congregation, they were undisturbed, for their work lay during the hours of sleep.

In the very centre of the altar steps was placed a large round vessel shaped rather like a chalice, with a cover, on which was graven the symbolic image of the Dove, symbol of the Holy Spirit of Love.

The vessel was covered during the hour of prayer, and the first hour of prayer was held at the noon-tide hour, roughly, on the day which we call Friday, that depending on the phases of the moon. Then a temple service of great beauty came into being, a service during which the assembled congregation watched the great Chalice being carried by those who served the Chalice to its place on the altar steps; where they watched the white-robed priests enter from behind the altar – one group on the right, the other on the left, and when all was ready the Temple curtains fell and from the gallery at the back came the great Bell, the image of the bell used in the Great Valley of Praise, with its massive brass notes and its strong clear tone.

A service of praise went forth and all contributed to it, and during the hour of the praise the priests' souls departed from their bodies and were raised through the roof of the temple to the place of light.

Those who have studied Egyptian healing will find many illustrations in the Egyptian tablets which show a man recumbent on a flat table-like structure and beside this recumbent figure two priests with arms stretched out, one arm out at the side and the other arm straight out in front, both on a level with the shoulders.

These priests are absolutely motionless and their duty was to remain thus until the soul-spirit had departed far enough for it to be away from their vision.

Then one on either side would stoop and kneel beside the recumbent figure, changing even as the court at your palace is changed every given number of hours, that the body of the priest was never left while the soul was absent.

Often people will say, 'This is the picture of the death of a man', or perchance will then say, 'This is the departure of the spirit from the body in trance.'

Neither is correct. These tablets are picturing for subsequent generations the departure of the soul of the priest when it returned to the Father-Mother God to gain light and love, power and glory, and above all the instructions of Ptah, that they might follow those instructions in the work and the service of the temple.

The service for the departing spirit held less importance than the service for the return of the soul spirit, which was of vital importance. We will return in thought to the temple again and watch from a distance what occurs.

We shall notice that the great curtains, the veils which you hear so often spoken of in the Bible, and which are so misunderstood by the man who reads his Bible, are completely alive with light. Every thread of the mesh is visible and it is that pure white light, the Pentecostal light of the soul purified, for a great purification has taken place through the sacrifice of the priests in withdrawing from the physical body to fulfil their service in the place of light.

The assembled congregation is great – much more numerous, for many more attend the return than the departure. Those who attend the departure are specially chosen, that they might give the right power to the departing soul-spirit.

The high priest and his two attendants come forward from behind the altar and the highpriest stands with both hands before him, palms uppermost, behind the great vessel with the symbolic Dove upon it, and on either side of it stand the two lesser priests, ready at the given symbol to raise the cover of the vessel.

There really is no need to raise the cover, for the vessel is already filled with that power of the spirit which has been brought back by the sleeping priests, the power of the love of God encased in the holy vessel, that it may be used on special occasions only, and handed only to those who have already learned how to use and how to accept the love of God at the hands of the highpriest.

But unless these symbols are observed and unless they were observed in Egypt, the people of Egypt would hardly have understood exactly what had taken place.

At the sound of the bell, as the great note goes forth, the lesser priests with reverence raise the lid and from the vessel comes forth the triple Flame, the Flame of the Pentecostal glory of the Father-Mother God, flame in which no dross, or ugliness can live, the love from the heart of Ptah.

This is the gift the priests have brought back from sleep. The lid is replaced and the Vessel is carried to a place upon the high altar and spirit hands place around it the golden radiance of the Golden Ray that it may be shielded now from the gaze of physical man.

The AUM is sounded throughout the temple and the gates open. The priests who have slept rise and stand beside their couches, bow their heads with humility and deep gratefulness before the altar; the congregation moves away, and at the command of the highpriest officiating, there come forward scribes who hold the tablets of the temple.

To each priest who has slept is allotted a scribe and the priest speaks to the scribe of the place wherein he has dwelt during the hours of sleep and the wonder of the experience.

And the hour is the hour of noon, on the day of Ptah, which is the Lord's Day.

To remember through many hours of sleep needs many years of training. Step by step the novice moves through all his periods of training and teaching in the temple, carrying the vessels which hold the honey and the wheaten bread and the milk for the students, sweeping the floors and working under this one and that in all the humble services of the temple and the temple servants, until there comes a moment when he is permitted at the hour of noon to sing the sound of 'Ah'. It takes a long time before he can reach the sound of 'Ah', which is the first note of God's love. Then the other notes that will have to be learned – 'Oh', 'Ooh', 'I', 'Ai,' 'Ee'.

When the menial service of the student is finished the mental training begins, the ritual movement and the dance, for in the temple dance every movement, even the movement of a finger, has a meaning which forms part of the ritual of the service itself. The learning of the power of light and the use of light and the power of colour and the use of colour, the power of sound and the use of sound, until one note melts into another, until a purity of notes is formed and an instrument chosen, for not only must the temple student learn to use every movement of the physical body in God's service, but he must learn also to use his eyes to see, his ears to hear, his voice to speak and sing.

Following that, the long period of training in the mirrors, the development of the gifts of the spirit, the acceptance with humility of the path, and here and there throughout the training the bitter taste, often failing, sometimes succeeding, before he can reach that moment, reached by the original Masters of the temple who came to earth with the gift, because they had the power within themselves of God to use it, the power to withdraw from the physical world, to leave the physical body quiescent and asleep, and during those hours of sleep to return to the place of light, and above all, to remember when you return.

How wonderful is that memory which comes after the long sleep, which is not the sleep of death but the sleep in life. It is the greatest gift of all, for it helps you to bring back the glory of the heavens and the power of the love of God and to use it in service to your fellow men.

CHAPTER TWENTY THREE

The Temple of the Ripened Corn

Many hundreds of the priests and highpriests of Atlantis reincarnated in Egypt. There were two distinct groups of temples, those connected with the court in which the kings were priests and the priests were kings, and those which were set aside, such as the Temple of Isis and others, in which only priestly work was carried out and in which there was no link at all with the court. These were temples of healing and teaching where young men and women were dedicated and prepared for the priesthood.

There came a day in one of these ancient priestly temples when a great desire made itself felt among the younger priests, that they should take into their hands a begging bowl and a staff and don a rough garment of camel's hair and go forth into the world. They were unaffected by any desire for power, or to see the world, or to join forces with material things; they merely felt within their hearts that some of that great power within these wonderful temples should be carried out into the world, as many pilgrims have felt before. And they gathered themselves into a group of brothers and they went to the high priest and they asked his permission to prepare themselves with humility and to go forth to teach the world of men about God.

This little band of men were those who had been used as channels for darkness in the gardens of Atlantis; therefore, although they held the light of the temple, they also held the capacity of darkness and the highpriest, although he gave permission, posted a special watcher in the roof of his temple so that he should guide the pilgrims as they went on their several ways and also, so that that watcher should report to him whether there were any who went astray. For those the highpriest would have sent out messengers to bring them back, that they might not go from his temple in such a way that they could hold the darkness instead of the light.

They were good for this task that they had taken unto themselves because they were children of the earth and the soil; they knew very little of the great places of the world and therefore they would not hanker after wealth, power, rich food, or women. They were merely workers, and as workers they went forth.

They divided themselves into four groups of three. Three were directed to a great desert in Lower Egypt. The watcher who stood in the pinnacle of the temple and watched their way and their progress was a young priest trained in astrology and able to read the signs in the Sun and the Moon and the Stars. He wore on his head a light casque which was kept in place by a band, the band descending on the forehead and covering that part of the head just above the ears, finishing at the back. This cap, and the band which held it, were magnetised from the rays of power within the inner sanctuary, so that in whichever direction he looked he was able without speaking, to report to the inner sanctuary the place of pilgrimage of each pilgrim who had gone forth.

The pilgrims were known by numbers, the numbers being quite unlike your numbers; in fact, you would have called them letters; they were the very early and simple letters which later became the hieroglyphs of Egypt.

The three who were directed to the desert found a lowly type of man tilling a hard way and endeavouring to grow corn under most difficult conditions. There was no rain, the sun was hot, far too hot, and as soon as they planted their grains the sun scorched and dried them up. The three pilgrims felt that they would not be able to help these vast numbers of poor field workers unless they could build a temple, and they had no idea how to build a temple, nor had they anything whereof to build it.

So they waited until the harvest and then persuaded these humble people to gather the straw from the harvest which was very poor, for the wheat had been planted many times before it had germinated at all, and with that straw, crushed by the action of the men's feet upon the stone to which it was pressed, mixed with water brought from a long distance, they made a kind of brick, and with that brick and a series of bricks they built a small circular temple rather like the igloo of the eskimo but much, much smaller. Within that temple the priests set up a statue of the God they worshipped and they told the people about God and they explained to them, that if they prayed to God He would make their lot easier and help them to grow their corn so that famine did not scourge their ranks and their children should live.

That tiny mud hut was the Temple of the Ripened Corn, for it had been built with immense labour out of the bricks made from the harvested straw, and they chose three fine heads of corn which they placed upon the altar of their God.

From the moment that it was erected, the lot of the people changed. Sickness left them and they came to the temple to thank God for their release, joy came into their hearts, especially joy in labour, until one day that tiny mud hut was left and a little further away was builded a wonderful temple, wonderful to them, though very simple to the eyes of men.

For the second temple they dug down into the sand and they made a great cavern below the temple, which became known as the Cavern of Initiation, where men had to go and prove to these pilgrims, who had become the priests of the temple, that they were ready and able to serve God, even more tangibly by the work of their hands in the fields, those sandy acres which you could hardly call fields.

It was a temple with foundations, and the pillars were erected and a dome was made and within the dome they placed a watcher, so that here in a much lesser degree they had a temple which was the replica of the temple which they had left.

That tract of Lower Egypt has become much vaster than it was in those days and towards that tract of land there has been directed a group of men who are well known as the Men of the Trees. They have planted trees in barren places throughout the world and they have planted trees now along this arid part which was the estate of the Temple of the Ripened Corn.

The trees they have planted are as yet few in number. A few pine trees planted from pine kernels, a few peach and nectarine trees from fruits which had been consumed by the planters during their stay in an Egyptian hotel.

So the Temple of the Ripened Corn is coming into its own again and a beauteous garden is made from the dark arid soil of the desert. It will be a long time before we shall see the real results of that planting. Perhaps we shall have to look down upon it from the other side of life, but surely and steadily that planting is going forward, and if you speak to the Men of the Trees, especially the leader, you will realise what a long way he has been led before he was considered able to prepare the soil in this particular land.

CHAPTER TWENTY FOUR

The Tomb of Akhnaton

Many souls who are incarnate today are incarnate from bodies which they held in the time of Akhnaton. Through study, meditation and concentration, at this moment the incidents in which we were concerned can be built through our ancient memory, and in remembering we may not only help to bring to light knowledge which will be of importance to the archaeologists and others, but also will link the path of our own soul with the paths of others who trod the self-same way with us during that particular Dynasty.

You believe that the tomb of Akhnaton has been discovered and all that was in it has been revealed. This is not so. His Tomb lies as yet untouched, undisturbed, three stories down below ground level of the Temple of Thebes. Many discoveries will be made of the first layer of that ancient Temple, much will be found of the second layer dealing with matters concerning the Great Atlantean Temple; then, at the third layer shall we find this vast and glorious Temple within which the body of Akhnaton is held in reverence and light.

For Akhnaton was, and is, a great soul; he is a Master loosed now in the spheres, to guide the rulers of the nations of the earth to peace. He was the son of Amen Hotep the Third and Queen Thitos was his mother; he was given the name of Amen Hotep and was, in reality, Amen Hotep the Fourth; at a later date he was surnamed Akhnaton. Therefore, his whole name was, in reality, Amen Hotep Akhnaton.

There was a great link between Amen Hotep the Fourth

and his mother, Queen Thitos – she came from a long way across the Tigris and belonged to a mighty nation. She had great strength of character, and intuition not only on earthly matters but of the things of the spirit, and through her intuition she guided the father of her son in the plans that he made for the ruling and governance of Egypt under the dual crown. She was imperious as a woman in such a position must be; there was most probably much in her life which she regretted, incidents which forced her into certain situations which disturbed her mind and life during its earthly tenure.

Amen Hotep the Fourth was guided from the age of ten by Oneferu, the Master who, incarnate in the body in that day of time, received and held the name of Menaton. Menaton, the High Priest, decided and planned the young king's studies. He conciliated Queen Thitos when she would put too heavy a burden upon the boy's shoulders; he trained him in discipline and courtesy and all the attributes of a prince of a noble house.

At the age of seventeen, Amen Hotep the Fourth met, during the court ceremony, a very beautiful girl. Her name was Hareth. They loved each other dearly and, under the guidance of the Father but against the wish of Queen Thitos, they became joint rulers of Egypt. But only for a few years, for the people of Egypt demanded that a Princess of a royal line should sit upon the Throne beside their King. Therefore, one was brought from a long distance whose beauty was of such glory and magnificence that it was believed the young King as soon as he saw her would reject Hareth and demand this Princess. The pressure of Queen Thitos, and of those in high positions in the court and temple decided that this Princess, Nefertiti, should become the joint ruler of Egypt. And it was so – but there was no love between the young Prince and the beautiful girl although she supported Akhnaton in his desire to see the worship of the one God carried out in all temples.

She was pliable and easily led by those who sought to gain power and position, and when she discovered that the young Prince had no love for her but that his sight and speech were directed ever to Hareth, she listened to those of the Court who insisted that she should steal or have stolen the son of Hareth

145

that he should reign as her son and later as a King in Egypt. In time he became known as Tutankamon, he died very young from syphilis.

The advice and admonition of Queen Thitos was at all times essential to Amen Hotep the Third – and later to her son Amen Hotep the Fourth; she commanded great canals to be made and built in Egypt and better houses for the workers in the fields and in the cities; she insisted that the King made arrangements for the gathering and the harbouring of the corn – for the winnowing of the corn, and for the use of the scales of justice to decide the wrongs of the people.

It was a strange soul – at times so hard, so strong; at times so weak where her devotion to her husband and her son led her – but at all times turned for the good of the people, for the building of places where children would be safe, for the building of homes for the people of the poor, for the building of dams for the irrigation of the country, and the right growing of the rice and the corn.

Throughout the reign of Amen Hotep the Third the building of the Temple of Thebes went forward – to all intents and purposes a surface temple, where girls were trained in the arts of the dance and movement and the reading of the mirrors and other temple service; where students and novices who had passed their tests in the temple service were led down vast staircases of stone built under the temple in the desert, where they passed through to yet another temple, lit by an inner glory of light, from the meditation of the great body of priests that served. These were all incarnated Atlantean priests, who had renounced the joy of the open air, the love of the trees which they brought from Atlantis, the love of the gardens and the direction of the great waters, to spend their lives in this subterranean temple to create the Light of the Father-Mother God within it.

In this temple, Queen Thitos worshipped – in the morning, at noon and eventide she said her prayers to the Priest of the Temple itself. She held the small flame, the candle of the Lord, that men might see and know that though there was daylight beyond, unless there was the Light of the Father-Mother God within the heart, all temples would be in darkness and in shadow.

The court in which Akhnaton found himself was composed of a large body of people who had no intention of being moved from their ancient rites and customs. He turned his attention to the temples and found that they were divided into two distinct types; the minority, where worship was favoured, where the records on marble were perfect, where all was in order, and the manifestation of spiritual gifts as God willed it; but in the other temples, as is the case in all ages, there was great darkness. There were priests who sought power, priests who sought glory, priests who sought to bend all men to their way of thinking and who were offering sacrifices which were wrong and which they had no right to offer in the land of Egypt.

Had Akhnaton turned to these and cleansed and purified them, the whole trend of history would have been different, but he did not confine his interests to the dark temples; he closed all temples and demanded that the Sun's disc should be worshipped.

These people were of simple habits and they loved the worship of Amen-Ra. Many of them were old and did not want to change to new customs. Many were quite prepared to give their assistance in all ways in the cleansing and the closing of the dark temples alone, but did not desire a new religion. So we see this young impetuous Pharaoh charging his way through the ancient customs of the people, urging and demanding a new worship and closing all temples, where seership was acknowledged as part of the Temple ritual.

He erected a new temple between the two great temples to Amen-Ra, where he introduced the worship of the one God; and the people were angered and would have none of this new worship, and so he took his court and all his temple followers a distance away, and there, at a place called Tell-el-Amarna, he erected a glorious temple and, at his command, a new service, new rites, new ritual serving Aton, the sun's disc, was fulfilled. Therefore, he aroused hatred in the hearts of his people, and although, as he grew older he would have given much to put the clock back and see the ancient temples and ancient rituals revived, this he could not do.

That is one side of the character of Akhnaton. Yet reform in certain Egyptian temples was vital and a call went out from

147

the planes of light that there should be found an instrument able to accept and hold the power which could be given to him for the cleansing and re-building of these temples of darkness. And Aknaton, who was indeed open to the voice of God, and who was indeed a pure channel at times for the power of spirit, knelt and prayed and said, 'Divine Father, show me thy will'.

The spirit which moved him, the spirit which pushed him forward to do the work at the bidding of our Father-Mother God, and substitute temples of light where were temples of darkness, and to throw out the evening sacrifices made by unenlightened priests, who sought only power and material gain for themselves, was good, but he was not content. The more he saw the wonderful vessels which had been collected by those who guarded the temples of darkness, the more did he desire to use even more wonderful vessels in the rites which he proposed.

He could have cleansed those temples with a great and mighty spirit, he could have poured the unquenchable flame of fire upon those places of darkness, but he went further and, instead of establishing a new and clean form of worship in the temples of darkness alone, he endeavoured to turn all men to the new religion.

As he began his purification in the temples of darkness, he appeared to the people as a new Christ, a Being of glory and strength and power, a mystic with beauty and light, standing at the crossroads of life and calling them to drink of the waters of eternity. Had he stopped there his work would have gone down through all time as a thing of glory.

To Akhnaton alone was granted the privilege of descent into the third temple which should later be his tomb, and here, under the guidance of Oneferu, he learned to meditate, to remain in the silence; he learned to send forth from within his heart so great a light of God, that the temple of the second degree and the temple of the first degree were lit alight from the glory of the third. And here he learned to walk bare-foot upon the rugged stones of the path to the Sanctuary; here he learned that all sacrifice which God demanded of him was of little worth without the strength and the opening of the heart. Here he learned the meaning of death, the reason for dying,

148

the reason for karma and reincarnation. Here he prepared tablets which gave his life and the life of his fathers, his previous lives on earth and the lives which were to follow, so that in that temple tomb lies the full record and statement of the lives of Menaton and he lives of Amen Hotep the Third; and of Amen Hotep the Fourth, Akhnaton. And all this in preparation not for the life which he lived in the body, not for the death he died in the spirit, not for the journey of the soul to paradise, but that when he returned into incarnation upon the earth plane again, he should be able to turn the tablets and see and mark and learn that he might not falter or fail in any place as he went forward.

Akhnaton, whose boyhood name was Amen Hotep – these words have power and should be pronounced slowly – watched and helped to build the tomb in which his body lies. Although the tomb is very deep below the level of the sea there is no sign of damp, or the ravages of water, of mildew, or the ravages of creatures. The tomb itself is of transparent stone, stone which was used in the great Temple of Atlantis and in Persia for the healing beds; in some lights it looks of one colour only; in others it looks of many colours; the rays of the Place of Light pass through it and enfold it, beating their power into the earth, drawing from the sand a great light and using it for the preparation of yet further rays, which will eventually guide those who hold the key to the tomb. None other may approach it.

The coffins, or sarcophagus, lie side by side with one another; in the one the magnificent figure of Akhnaton and the other the figure of Hareth; and that you may know she is Hareth when you hear of her finding, you will remember that about the brow she bears a golden circlet, wide, soft, which though restraining the tresses it leaves no impress upon the delicate brow itself. In the centre of that golden band is a mighty ruby, shining as no ruby you have ever seen shone before. The hands are delicate, cared for and beautiful.

The body of Hareth beside the body of Akhnaton look as they looked in life – no decomposition, no fading of the tissue, no darkening of the colour of the skin, for the preservation of these bodies is perfect; only when the light of day strikes them

149

do they crumble into dust. But they will not crumble until their proof is established and all those who have the right to do so have been permitted to look upon the features of one of the greatest and the most important Kings of the earth, whose soul left the Place of Light and through many incarnations reached the body of a Prince, to serve as a King and to pass back to the Place of Light again.

For to understand our past lives we must pray to Akhnaton; he has the clue; sometimes that information will be passed through to you by your doorkeeper, or by someone who is permitted for you to read the Akashic record of the past; but only to those who hold the Silver Ankh in a certain position as proof that they have the right to read it, only to these will be given the privilege and the power.

Outside the tomb at either end will be discovered two small chambers, so small that a man would have difficulty in standing upright therein – but these are merely boxes of records. In the box placed at the head of the young King and Hareth will be found a manuscript in ancient script giving the clue to the last Books of *Genesis*; in the other will be found a script in Aramaic, but written long before anyone speaking Aramaic or writing Aramaic upon the tablets approached the Court of Egypt. These scripts will need special readers, only one or two, who have been trained under the guidance of Oneferu, will be able to read them, only these will be able to place them in their proper position in the Book of *Genesis* and in that last book which should follow the writing of the *Revelation of St. John* – the book which closes that book of Scriptures which you know as your Bible.

The pathway to the tomb is in darkness; men must traverse the temple and many passages before he reaches the tomb; and the passages are sown with white stones – the white stone representing the Light of the Spirit, stones just large enough for a man to hold in the palm of his hand. When the right man treads the passage the stones lift, the light shines and he walks forward to the tomb itself, where he will be called upon to worship, for God in His Holiness is the guide and strength of mankind, the director of the life of man and the mighty works of God.

CHAPTER TWENTY FIVE

The Temple of Thebes

The court of Egypt was a very large one, and we are approaching the moment when the revelations of the past will be made plain to man; the revelations about Atlantis and the life of Atlantis must be proved to the student and the archaeologist and all who are concerned with the past history of the world. We have discussed certain points and you will look to those who make the necessary discoveries to prove those points to you, for the history of Egypt depends upon the revelation of Atlantis and the revelation of our day depends upon the history of Egypt. Therefore, every detail from the most minute pin which is found on the floor of a tomb in ancient Egypt, to the colour of the blossom of one of the great trees in the gardens of Paradise; on the texture of the net of which the curtains in the Temple of Atlantis were woven, to the texture of the linen which you use for your priestly garments today; all this depends upon every point in the past and every point in the present fitting exactly rightly and with truth.

For this revelation was given by the ancient prophets; it is the revelation which was given in the *Book of Revelation* by St. John, on the Island of Patmos, and just as that pin which is discovered in the tomb of a Queen of Egypt depends for the knowledge which is brought to bear upon it, on what has preceded its placement and what has caused the searchers to find it; so every incident of these great prophecies, symbol for symbol, picture for picture, line, word, note and touch depend upon all that has taken place between the building of the Atlantean Temple and the excavation of the Egyptian tomb today.

We live in a dangerous age, an age when the black magic which was used in Egypt is abroad in all its intensity because those who rule the darkness do not wish the light to prevail and, therefore, where they can use their art, their magic to prevent the light penetrating and holding sway, they will do so. Sometimes that darkness penetrates through Governments, and kings and rulers; sometimes it is only manifest through the individual sins of the personality, in individuals working for God in the flesh today.

But the darkness knows no night or day; it is alive and awake at all times and ready and able to touch you particularly, because you have dwelled in the Egyptian temple; you have seen the black arts practised; you have shared the common sacrifice and away back in your own past memory lies the knowledge which you have spent incarnation after incarnation to throw aside. You see this darkness penetrating in the use of atomic energy for warfare, you see it penetrating through cruelty to animals, to men, women and children; you see it in the desire to develop the things of the spirit quickly, rapidly, by means of drugs – and these drugs are not confined only to the seekers after illumination – they are being used more and more for curing disease, or so-called cures of disease. The effects of these drugs react upon the physical body and where they take away pain in one place they sow disease in another. You see serums made from cattle injected into young children and all round you see the darkness gloating with the minions and the servants it has obtained. Here and there you have wonderful men who are instruments of the light, who bring this knowledge of the light to mankind through the knowledge of homoeopathy and biochemics and natural methods of healing. But you see the whole of your country in the stranglehold of a system which is described as National Health – a system which is used with circumspection by the darkness, hitting, striking, damaging where it can – but not always from the negative angle, curing first and through those cures effected, it may gain bi-partisan workers and helpers. A young doctor finishing his qualification sees the immediate effect of a drug on a child patient and studies that drug that he may use it to gain the same effect, and so it goes on.

We band together in a small group, God-loving people, to destroy the works of darkness, by planting the seeds of light in the human soul, by achieving cures of healing which are not spectacular, which are slow in working and which adapt the physical body – while curing the disease – to the power of the light. And not only us; hundreds of other groups all over the world are doing the same, sitting in meditation and teaching their students to meditate in light. And here, now and again, you find intellectual people at the top of their intellectual tree, putting forth theories, psychic development, by means of drugs, through carelessness, through wrong sitting, which can destroy the work of God. They are not openly wicked, and if we were to tell them that they are assisting that very darkness which they did their utmost to prevent in Egypt, they would be stricken and horrified. The work that they do is done unconsciously but the damage that it does is as great as ever.

So we return in thought to Akhnaton; we see his bitter sorrow when the news is brought to him of the death of Hareth, the Mother of his son, for Hareth linked with Akhnaton in the great Atlantean Temple on the Heights; neither had in any day stooped to the dark sacrifice which others who surrounded Akhnaton in the Court had stooped to fulfil.

Menaton, high priest of the Court of Akhnaton knew the innermost secrets of the King's heart, and he truly, with the direction of the Father-Mother God, knew exactly what had to be undertaken by Akhnaton in the fulfilment of the Law of God, for no man is king by the order of men only, man is king by the command of God, and God gives to that kingly soul a work of special importance in the world in which he lives, the kingdom over which he rules; that work is hidden and unseen; it is fulfilled under the guidance at all times of a great high priest, sometimes that highpriest is discarnate, sometimes he is twin-soul incarnate, but he is always at the side of a kingly ruler who is appointed by God to fulfil some work for man.

153

Part of the work that Akhnaton had to do was to leave behind him, when he passed to the world of spirit, certain proofs of what he had brought through his own memory, from his own life as a high priest in Atlantis, so that the history of Atlantis could be proved at the right moment, and that moment would be when the revelation commanded, that the tomb of Akhnaton should be discovered and the completion of his work given to the world.

Besides the tomb, Akhnaton built a very great temple at Thebes; it was a temple into which gathered the highpriests of all the nations of the world, a temple where the astrologers from the East came for power and understanding. Therefore, astrology was much studied at the court of Pharaoh; the conversation at the banquets and all reunions in the palace were of astrological signs and symbols and, therefore, it was not remarkable that, also it was ordained by God, that there should be men and women at the Court of Akhnaton who could read the astrological signs and symbols, not as prophecy, but as the necessary symbols to be placed in the tomb of Akhnaton when it was prepared for his burial, symbols which would be read by the astrologers of today and tomorrow, understood by them and give proof of the conditions of life in Atlantis; of the glory of the Temple on the Heights, of the simple beauty of that first valley life and of the darkness which crept in and its destruction.

So that whereas outwardly the life of Akhnaton was the life of a ruler of his people and a ruler who understood the people of Egypt who worked for them, who knew what he was doing under the guidance of Menaton, under the guidance of God, who prepared the way for them but who knew also that a certain time each day must be given to meditation in the company of the priest, that in that meditative hour he might learn from the Father-Mother God Himself the progress of his work, progress which at times, to this impetuous young king seemed slow and yet because he trusted Menaton, he fulfilled every step without faltering, or failing.

In that great Temple of Thebes we see the preparation made for the training of the lookers, the bringing to the temple of girls to be dedicated for the dance – not dance as you know

154

it but the graceful, glorious movements to the temple music, where instruments of an unusual nature, hardly known to man today, were in use and where girls were trained and educated in the temple service and learned to read the mirrors. This was not for the fortunes of the people of the Court – they only did that when darkness crept in, then were they destroyed – but to read the mirrors, that they might watch the fulfilment of the prophecies of the ancient prophets, Daniel, Isaiah, and all the others, and then coming from later times to the prophecy of St. John, already built in a picture upon the ether, prepared for the study of kings, not yet played for the minds of men.

As soon as the great tomb of Akhnaton was begun – three floors below the level of the sand of the desert – there came a great and mighty rush of workers in black magic; they came both from the East and West and they used a very powerful force, for they impressed their thought upon the souls of those whom they wanted to influence.

It is only possible for anyone to impress the thought on the *ka*, or soul of the person himself. Therefore, if the great one who should be influenced after his death is buried in a place unknown and his place in the tomb prepared for him is taken by a faithful steward, or member of the household, who is destined for that particular work in the fulfilment of the service of God, the darkness cannot impress itself upon the soul of the great one. The darkness could not affect the body of Akhnaton, if the body upon which it was working was in reality the body of the steward. Thus came into force in that period of Egypt a great and mighty practice, the burial of a steward, or some member of the Court, who should be given the important place of the burial of the king; that the steward should be placed in a tomb worthy of the reception of the mummy – or body of a king – but that the true body of the king should be placed in another tomb guarded and sealed by the powers of light, so far down in the centre of the earth, that the darkness was unable to reach it. But the darkness could not easily be taken in; therefore the tomb of the steward must be equal in all respects to the tomb of the king; all that it lacked was certain symbols which were essential to the history

155

of the king, which proved the prophecies of the present and linked them with the prophecies of the past.

So when the time comes – and it will only come at the right moment in the history of mankind, when all things are ready, for the book of life to be read – the tomb of Akhnaton will be opened and there will be the two bodies there, side by side. There will be certain symbols; on the brow of Hareth will be the golden band and the great ruby in the centre, and at her feet will be a tiny bag of golden tissue, which contains the crimson scarabs of Atlantis; the statue – two statues – of Akhnaton stand erect at the feet of the bodies; these statues are built and, though they are gilded, are an exact likeness of the King taken from two different angles. As you descend the stairs into the tomb you will notice that though their faces appear to be identical because one statue is turned to the right and the other to the left, the features appear different. These statues are robed in linen and, in spite of thousands of years, it has not decayed, and is as strong and pure and as white as the day it was placed as the covering garment of the King. Certain symbols, which we are not yet permitted to disclose, are broidered upon the breast of the robes of both statues and in each broidery there is a minute portion missing, so that when the two broidered parts are placed together the pattern is perfect – single it is imperfect. The gold leaf which covers the feet of the King show every vein in the foot, every mark of the nails and it is these two statues which will prove the identity of the body of the King himself. At his feet there lies a circlet formed of circular stones, every precious stone which has ever existed in the world is in that circlet, and this circlet will be discovered at the moment when the prophecies of St. John become plain to the scholars of mankind.

CHAPTER TWENTY SIX

The Contrast between Egypt and Assyria

In Assyria there was a powerful priesthood entirely ruled by the court; the words of the King of Assyria controlled the minds of the priests. Hence we see material life controlling the spiritual. At no time has God ever advocated the dominance of matter; He has always stated that man is spirit and that spirit within the soul must control the body. And if that is the case, matter may not therefore control spirit, nor the regulation of the life of spirit which is done by the priests.

If you read a history of Assyria, whether it be a simple book written for a child, or an important historical volume, you cannot but be struck by the incredible wealth and power of the kings of Assyria, of their courtiers, their queens, their sons and their daughters – arrogance and power predominated. Therefore the beauty of the spiritual life was shut down and unrealised. In fact, if you had been able to speak to any member of the great Assyrian Court about the things of the spirit, he would have given you a very different picture from that which we have today.

There were mediums in Assyria, tellers of the future, astrologers, but they were used only from the material angle, never from the spiritual. Quite the contrary existed in Egypt, for in Egypt it was the great and mighty temples of the spirit that dominated the court and the court-life until those moments came, when the human sacrifices were made. But at all times would the Kings of Egypt listen to the voice of the

157

highpriest; the glory of the Egyptian temple was the light and radiance of God and the esoteric teaching was veiled to all who were not ready for it, and in its turn it veiled the truth; but the truth was there, visible to those whose ears were tuned in to hear it and whose hearts were ready to receive it.

Therefore, the history of the Egyptian priesthood is a very different history from that of the Assyrian priesthood and the history of the Egyptian court, from the history of the Assyrian court, because whereas the Assyrians sought to make the priests their vassals, the Egyptians sought to make their priests servants of God.

The presence of the medium in an Egyptian temple was of vital importance. The medium's life was guarded, cared for, arranged in such a way that she was free to go and come as she wished and where she wished but at all times she remembered, not that she was a servant of the temple, but a servant of the Most High God, to do His Will through the manifestation of the gifts of the spirit, in the guidance of the priests and the students and the novices in the temple, for the service of the temple alone.

Working with the medium in the Egyptian temples there were the lookers, and whereas the medium would read the future when commanded by the highpriest from the spiritual angle, for the regeneration of the race and the strengthening of man spiritually, the lookers were called upon to guide both priesthood and court by their method of reading the mirrors.

Some students may remember the great Temple of Osiris, where every second pillar contained a tiny cabinet and where the opening of the cabinet in every pillar was different from the last pillar, and the opening was known only to the looker who used or was called upon to use that particular group of mirrors; when moved, the tiny catch released the spring and the door swung back. It was a small square hole about twelve inches and at the back of it was fixed a mirror of a given dimension. There was a horizontal mirror of the same quality and dimension, fixed in the floor of the cabinet and when the lookers were trained they were taught to look in the perpendicular mirror, while the question that they asked was given in picture form in the horizontal mirror.

The training of these women was arduous and long because they had to learn so to control their thoughts, that they would not project upon the mirrors their own ideas or will; any looker who looked for the answer in the horizontal mirror, would most surely be horrified to find that instead of the blank mind on which the guiding spirit worked there was her own mind mirrored in the mirror itself, instead of the question that she had been asked to submit for the spirit to answer.

The lookers were not on the same level of consciousness as the medium and, therefore, today you find, not so many now as ten or twenty years ago, very large numbers of mediums who you would describe as astral mediums perhaps, or mediums working on an ordinary or low level of consciousness; who are in reality descendents, or reincarnated from the lookers in the temple and who follow the training that they received in the temple as a looker. Egypt as a civilization lasted very much longer than Assyria, due entirely to the power of the spirit which had been used, had been projected, had held so closely the esoteric secrets of truth in the ancient past.

There is one other point which is important in connection with the Egyptian civilisation and that was the inundation of the land by the Nile, at the time of the summer solstice. This was due entirely to natural conditions which occurred, not in Egypt itself, but in the adjoining country of Abyssinia; there among the mountains the rainfall was stupendously heavy during those weeks preceding the summer solstice and by the time the solstice was opening in Egypt, the great waters were pouring down – the result of the rainy season in Abyssinia – to swell the Nile and cause it to overflow its banks.

Physically the irrigation of the land for the growing of rice was magnificent – it was part of the life of the people, it was something for which they prepared, for which they prayed, and on which they depended for their source of life. These inundations also controlled the bird and animal life of the country surrounding the Nile. They enabled these vast quantities of papyrus grass to be grown for the making of the parchment and many other things connected with the temple and the court.

159

Although the making of the Delta of the Nile did not occur until many hundred years later, it was the direct result of the inundations at the time of the summer solstice which washed tons of sand from one place to another; and, under the burning heat of the sun, brought the moist humid climate to the people.

Some of Egypt's finest temples by the Nile were destroyed. The one which many students link with today, the Temple of Philae, is largely submerged. It was a beautiful temple built of quartz and pale pink marble, its great pillars after the Grecian style – flat roof holding the sunshine, and round the temple the great walk of the priests. You would call this walk in a temple today the cloisters – stone paved, the walls entirely of mosaic although they were not called mosaic in Egypt. The Italians copied the tesselated walls from the Egyptians and all the glory of the Sun over the sea, for this temple was on a tongue of land which jutted out into the sea.

What wonderful training and service was prepared in that temple and how many of us think of it with joy and with longing to see it recreated from the past again today.

The only heritage we have from Egypt that we ourselves live with and understand is the Sphinx. And how the words of Hermes are borne out when he said to Aescalapius, 'Oh, Egypt, Egypt, how we shall mourn thee, for nothing shall be left but thy tablet of stone.' Let us look at the Sphinx; partly bull, partly lion, partly man, partly eagle – the four creatures described in the *Book of Ezekiel* borne out in Egypt, borne out again in the *Book of Revelation*, and some of us belong to that past, which we remember when we feel the sands of the desert warm under our feet.

CHAPTER TWENTY SEVEN

An Initiation in the Twentieth Egyptian Dynasty

We are now considering a period 1300 years before the birth of Christ. The Pharaohs of the 20th Egyptian Dynasty were reigning and we are called upon to assist in the replaying of the karmic condition of that period.

When we are engaged in playing out a karmic condition in cycle, the conditions of the past must be replayed under identical signs and planets as occurred during the period itself. Therefore if we were able to make a chart of the Temple of Thebes at that particular moment, we should find that the stars and the planets had exactly the same bearing and influence upon each other as the planets and stars have upon us today, with one exception, that today we are further afflicted by the planet Pluto.

If we examine the building of the Temple of Thebes, we shall find one main central Sanctuary; and around it, close built against its walls, the twelve smaller communicating sanctuaries which feed and protect, or rather fed and protected the Mother Sanctuary and collected power from the Mother Sanctuary for their upbringing and evolution.

The time that we are touching is the time of the greatest strife in Egypt, when Egypt was beset by the Assyrians, the Babylonians and Amalekites. The Egyptian Pharaoh went forth with his servants and his students, his sword carriers and his shield bearers to protect the Ark of the Covenant, which contained the precious stone upon which all esoteric teaching throughout all the ages of man is founded. That stone was of marble, translucent and transparent, holding within its heart all the colours of the spectrum, collecting from the surrounding ether all rays and colours that can be used in the art of healing, collecting from the greater places of the ether the extraordinary power of the rays required for the vanquishing of the enemies of God.

And upon this stone, inscribed by an Atlantean high priest, was the whole of the symbolic teaching which we are endeavouring in our turn to unravel and to understand today, seeking little by little to tread the path of peace, with the knowledge of those great lives of the past, who built the foundation of the Ark of the Covenant of the Lord. That stone was the precious burden which the Israelites carried into the wilderness, which they defended with their very lives and brought to rest upon Mount Sinai.

The time we are considering is the time of Moses and Orpheus, and if you study the life of Moses you will realise that much of the teaching is symbolically inclined towards the teaching of Egypt.

In their endeavour to defend their country from the invaders, the Egyptians built mighty roads towards the Lebanon, preparing the way for those who preceded the Master Jesus upon those roads, preparing also, in the same cycle of evolution in the time of the Master Jesus, giving meaning to the fact that the parents and the young child were caused to flee into Egypt and from Egypt to return to the Lebanon; it was not accidental that the road of the parents and child was made smooth by the Egyptian forerunner. They built great forts to defend their land; though the forts are in ruins and their foundations difficult to discern, the power which they held is still there, for the Egyptians were not fighting only with hands and armour, they were fighting with the power of God held within their hearts, poured out in His service, that great incalculable unknown, unseen Being of Light.

While all this was going on in the great countries of the world a strange pilgrim approached the Temple of Isis; he was worn and weary and he broke his journey when the temple came in sight at the hut of a humble tiller of the soil. The tiller of the soil gave him meat and drink and lathed his feet in the waters of the Nile and prepared his own humble couch for his resting place, and cared for him and fed him until he was strong enough after the long and weary journey he had undertaken, to present himself before the doorkeeper of the temple itself.

The moment came when the postulant was received by the hierophant who took his two hands in his, placed them together upon the palm of his own left hand, placed the three fingers of his right hand upon the third eye in the centre of the forehead, and as he placed the fingers of his right hand upon the third eye, there rose around them a great singing of birds, the great glory of the blessing of God, brought to the first candidate for initiation in the Temple of Isis, the temple of the twelve subsidiary temples, the temple where all men served with gladness and with joy from the greatest highpriest to the most simple sweeper of the floors. Besides the singing of birds, there arose music round the bodies of the two men and where the fingers of the hierophant had rested came forth light, light of such golden glory as could hardly be expressed in words.

The postulant knelt at the feet of the hierophant and bowed his head and placed the palms of his hand upon his feet in token of complete obedience, complete submission to the will of God, complete submission to the law, and the hierophant said 'follow me', and the postulant followed and they came to an outer court in the temple where the hierophant handed over the postulant to the attendant who waited; and they took him to a cleansing and lathing temple, where in a bath of black marble he was prepared to take the initiation in the great Temple of Thebes.

Following the cleansing he was given honey to eat and milk to drink, and an egg in his right hand, and he was clothed in a simple garment of brown flax, woven from the outer skin and the leaves of the flax stems, harsh to the skin and dry. He was then blindfolded and led into the temple where the hierophant with five servants anointed his brow with oil, the centre of his head with oil, placed his right forefinger upon his lips in token that he must not speak a single word from the beginning to the end of the test; then, walking slowly out of the temple he beckoned the postulant to follow him.

They descended steep, grey stone steps to the bottom and here the postulant was given a lamp which had to be held with the right forefinger and the right thumb, the little finger placed underneath the base of the lamp, and he was told to go forward. The heavy door clanged behind him and he found himself alone.

Little by little as his eyes became used to the darkness, he saw that he was in a great chamber. On either side of him in rows down either side were the figures of men with the heads of beasts, each one representing an Egyptian Deity. By the light of the lamp he turned to the figure on the right and bowed low, placing the palms of his hands on the feet; and he did this down the right side of the temple to every figure and then returned he to the left side of the temple, to the place in which he had first stood. Here, his lamp went out and he stumbled forward, slowly and with hesitation to the place where he believed the door should be and when he reached it, he knocked thrice and the door opened and he found himself in a narrow passage way through which he had to pass. Above his head was a moving instrument which he could not see but which as he took every step, measured his step; it moved forward again giving him thus permission to move forward also.

It is from this instrument that are taken your circular doors and your turnstiles of today; so that when you pass through one of these circular doors in any of your great shops, or place of business, you will realise that you are touching the place of the candidate for initiation in the Egyptian mysteries.

A dim light shone before him and the hierophant, holding a lighted lamp, met him; no word was spoken, only the touch of his hand on the hand of the postulant and they went forward. They came to another doorway and through that doorway there burned a great and mighty furnace with leaping flames, no smoke. The hierophant motioned to the postulant that he must go forward through the flames and the latter fell on his knees beseeching that he might be spared this terrible ordeal; and the hierophant went behind him and placed his two

164

hands on his shoulders and urged him forward and except for the flames the candidate was in darkness and alone. With halting steps he went forward and as he reached the furnace, the furnace opened and parted and on either side of him the flames became living perfumed roses – the white rose which was to be his token of completion of initiation high above his head; on the right hand the red roses; on the left the pink, later adopted as the symbol of Pythagoras.

Through the furnace the hierophant again met the postulant and pointed to him the dark water which he must traverse. Again the postulant was afraid, having so little faith in the protection of God; after passing through the furnace in such a miraculous way, he shrank back from the lake, with its slime and its ugliness and the heads of dark monsters peeping through the surface of the slime; and again the hierophant urged him forward and again he found himself alone and in darkness. He longed to sleep but he dared not delay and eventually he went forward; it was not a pleasant experience, but when he had traversed the lake half way and his garments were clogged with the mud through which he had passed he saw at the other end a light held by the hierophant. He tried to hasten his steps, but he stumbled, and as he stumbled the light went out; as he raised himself the light appeared and he went forward again to the border of the lake and there, met by the hierophant, he knelt and gave thanks.

This was the last test except the mental test, and it is the mental tests that are written on the stone of the Ark of the Covenant; these were yet to come, but they are of the inner mysteries and are never spoken of except between the hierophant and the postulant at the third stage of initiation.

Here, in the sublimation of matter to God, we realise with strength and power how glorious was the understanding of the postulant who had passed the tests, how great was his rejoicing when he was handed the papyrus upon which was written the rest of his examination, the purpose of his examination, and the history of his place in the Universe of God and in the plan of God for the future of man.

CHAPTER TWENTY EIGHT

The Second Stage in the Neophyte's Initiation

After the neophyte had passed the first initiation, in spite of all the darkness and the suffering which he had been through in his search for the rock, which was to prove his own foundation stone, he still had to go through many trials and difficulties to complete the further stages of initiation. We see him coming forth feeling victorious, realising that he has completed something of note that marked a post, a turning post almost, in the career of his own life, a life of the soul as a whole from its creation to its return, to be enfolded in the eternal grace.

The second part of the initiation concerns death and resurrection, a state through which all men must pass, both in the material body and in the spiritual one, for man must pass death and resurrection through every plane of consciousness as he descends from the Place of Light to be born anew in a body of flesh as a tiny child; he must therefore suffer death and resurrection through every stage, or completion of a stage of his uprising and his beginning.

This second stage is not easy, but the neophyte has already become strong by all that he has faced fearlessly in those first tests. We will therefore watch him as he goes forth in the plain brown habit of the student, side by side with his guide and master, the hierophant.

Together they descend a vast number of stone steps, hearing the sound of running water on the left. There is nothing but silence on the right. The neophyte is led into a tiny stone cell, much smaller than the novice had in her convent incarnation. He comes forth from this cell at regular intervals to be instructed in meditation; this part of his initiation is hard because he is given no guidance at all; if he asks for a clearer vision for the path ahead of him, or a description of the next stage after this one, the hierophant merely replies 'wait and work'.

So we see him undertaking many so-called menial tasks, gathering sticks, preparing fires, carrying water, cleansing stones, and he becomes exceeding weary and longs for the light of day; he longs for the vision, the spiritual power which he believes is just beyond his vision. Neither come near him, then comes the day when weary and tired of this eternal sameness of life, the loneliness shut away in a cell to meditate hour by hour; and he asks the hierophant, 'Shall I ever breathe the scent of the rose of Isis and see the glory of her light?' And the hierophant says to him. 'That is not for us to tell you, you can only touch these things of glory by the development of your own soul. Go back and meditate. Wait and work. Remember that you are now on the path in which you will study complete and perfect truth – you are really standing in the Halls of Truth although your own soul is only on the threshold of it. Come, I will show you the Book of Life.'

He leads the student by the hand to a great desk whereon is a mighty book and he turns to the page inscribed with the student's celestial name; the student has never heard this name before and yet it moves him strangely, touches him in the hours of sleep and when he wakes he hears the name called. 'What are these writings? What are these symbols?" he asks.

'These symbols portray the story of your life, my son', said the hierophant, 'and there will come a day when you will have completed all that you are called upon to complete. Before you return to the Place of Light, you will read this book through with me and it will give the history of your own life from the very inception of the first birth down to the moment when, having completed the resurrection, you will be glorified in the Light of the Lord."

And the student says, 'This is all very well, I thought I knew

167

truth'. 'No man can know truth', replied the hierophant, 'until he has proved it from within himself; where his conscience is dark, where he has erred in a lie, where he has hurt another by reason of his own weakness; all these will act as barriers on the road to truth until the student himself, standing firmly upon the rock which he has prepared, opens his soul to God and brings out in all their ugliness the faults of his personality which are the barriers to the lightening of the consciousness and the perfection of the soul of power.'

The neophyte went on in the same way day by day, drawing a little nearer to the glory of the passing and day by day instead of puffing himself up and feeling a very superior person, finding himself more humble and less near the truth than he seemed to be at the beginning. It was only when he came to kneel in deep humility, on the cold hard stone he had prepared for the foundation of his temple, when he called to the hierophant to mirror upon the wall before him his own character he is now discovering and was ready to produce to discuss with the hierophant, he realised where he had gone wrong and how much untruth had barred his way.

It is not an easy thing to unfold your character on the steps of the altar before the priest, but this he did, and many moons passed before he had completed the examination which through the very power of God surrounding him, showed him where his ugliness of soul lay.

He was taken by the hand and led into a chamber where one small light burned in the centre of the floor. To the left, the feet to the east, lay a great couch, the coverings were superb – silk, damask and gold – and the feet of the bed were long above the bed and turned round so that they were carven in the heads of lions.

Here, the neophyte, weary of his vigil lay down to rest, and his rest became a dream and the dream became a nightmare and he found himself engulfed in horror, black waters moved over his head, stars and planets left their courses and dropped around him a fiery furnace, and his feet were heavy as lead, his stomach sank for he had had no food, his voice appeared weak as he called for help and then the nightmare ceased and he slept.

It was a long sleep, for the sleep which follows the passing soul when the body is cast away to return to the dust of the earth and the soul itself wings its way to God, is a long wait and things seem unreal; the student found he was neither in the world, nor out of the world; he felt the weight of his physical body which endeavours to draw him back to the earth by the power of the personality; he felt the call of the soul to the Place of Light and before his eyes he saw the great Temple of Isis and the altar, the branches of roses upon the altar, and the perfume reached him not as a satisfaction, tantalising him, teasing him, because he longed for it and could not fulfil his longing.

The vision passed and he felt the weight of the physical body upon the bed, the couch was no longer a place of rest, he realised the glory and the beauty of his experience which seemed but a dream – no! no dream, for as he came back to life the Great One stood beside him – 'Son of man, thou who art also a son of God, thou hast called thyself, be with me in the Place of Light – you must journey through many planes of consciousness before the light of the spirit can touch the heart and the truth which thou desirest can be held as a ball of light in thy hand, but thou hast fulfilled.'

And beside the bed, moving round him and above him were clouds such as he had never before seen, for they were soft and white and yet of many colours; they moved swiftly but did not speak of haste; they were filled with the Glory of God in that dark place, and the neophyte lay and gradually the clouds grew together and from the centre of the cloud came forth a hand of exceeding beauty and it touched his brow and the perfume of the roses was left upon his brow, and it touched his lips and he felt no more would he cause untruth in the world, by the untruth of his own inner being, for the fingers burned his lips and the lips were scorched, though the perfume of roses of Isis remained behind.

The hand stretched forth he held and gradually the figure came out of the clouds, the figure of truth and beauty, peace, which waited for him; the figure became a living, breathing soul, one he knew and had known in many lives. He remembered that in other lives at the moment of death, he had

169

waited for her beyond the bridge of death and welcomed her gently, even as she welcomed him; and the clouds of glory enfolding them both – did not in any way lighten the great dark chamber – the lamp had gone out.

The neophyte remembered the hours he had spent in the great hall, studying the hieroglyphs, working with masters, and he remembered the menial work he had done in the cleansing of cells and passages, he remembered the loneliness when he was shut away in that tiny cell, to learn to speak with God. And as he remembered, it all fell away behind him and the vision led him forward, and the walls seemed to part – there was no door and yet these great stones rolled apart, even as they rolled apart from the entrance to the sepulchre. The neophyte stepped out into the light of day, proven in truth.

He asked, 'Where do we go now? Where am I?' The figure said, 'Thou art with me, thou hast crossed the bridge of death, thou art ready now to study all things in life; in this apparent tomb-like existence thou hast studied the sciences of the trees and the minerals and all the things of nature, thou hast studied the life of man, the history of the Gods, the beginning of time, the creation of the world, all these things thou knowest; although they do not appear as words upon thy lips, they are there in thy heart, thou would use them in the upliftment of mankind when the moment comes.

'For the great earth-mother has given thee much, thou hast suffered in the physical body in the world of men, thou hast sacrificed, thou hast been poor and in trouble, thou hast been joyous and in glory and all these things have shown thee the pathway of the soul; and those studies thou leavest behind – the studies of the spirit lie before thee; thou shalt now adjourn to the great bath and the clean white robe of the initiate and then I will meet thee and lead thee to the Hall of Learning, where the great vision of Hermes shall be unfolded before thy sight.

'Watch and pray. Thou hast been told to wait and work, thou hast been told to work and pray – now, watch and pray.'

CHAPTER TWENTY NINE

Moses and the Teaching of Monotheism

The little chamber behind the High Altar of the Temple of Osiris held the secret teaching – the esoteric teaching of the Most High God. There was a period in which the teaching of a monotheistic nature was given within that chamber and held there like the esoteric teaching of another order in secret. Only the priests had access to this. It was the teaching which must be given out following the teaching of many Gods that there should be one God – later to be called Jehovah – who should rule and guide the children of the earth.

On the 21st August, the Autumn Equinox of the earth plane is celebrated in the Place of Light. It was at this Equinoxial period that the greatest monotheistic teaching was given forth to those who served the priesthood in the Temple of Osiris. One of those priests, a young man, tall and handsome, graceful in carriage, strong in the arm, with a vision beyond his years, was to be found among the priests who served the secret chamber. This young man was an initiate, one of the greatest initiates who ever dwelt awhile in the body of flesh – his name was Moses. As so many initiates are called to do, he was of humble parentage, hidden by his mother at the command of the Most High God, in a cradle of rushes in the waters of the Nile and found there – not by chance, although it seemed so upon the earth, – by the daughter of the reigning Pharaoh – a child who had never been gainsaid since her birth, who had always demanded what she wanted and received it. Therefore, although it would appear unseemly for the daughter of Pharaoh to adopt an unknown child, it was permitted and the child was reared and educated in the palace and at the age of ten years dedicated to the priesthood.

At that period of time there were large numbers of nomadic people wandering through North Africa, back into Asia and round again through Egypt and beyond; they called themselves Bedoni – they are now called Bedouin. They were very simple people, rather like gypsies, who cared nothing for standards of living, who were prepared to serve under group leaders in groups, and to do what they were bidden, living from hand to mouth, their only vehicles asses and camels, and journeying always in that same cycle of time round through Asia and back through Egypt, North Africa and back to Egypt again. They camped, but their camping was short; they lived in tents of skins and they lived roughly; they were not very clean; they had very few standards and what standards they had were the standards of their faith and their faith rested in their leader.

Numbering many thousands they were divided under leaders with special names; they had their own banners and they were known as the twelve Tribes. Moses in his studies into monotheism knew from the guidance he received from the Place of Light, that it would be his task to unfold the doctrine of the one God in the world of men. He was a cautious man, not one who would plunge into any project without a great deal of thought. He must therefore experiment; how would this doctrine of monotheism, taken from the secret chamber of the Egyptian Temple, be accepted by any of the people with whom he moved and served as priest? He knew not at all and therefore he searched for a people, or a group of people through whom he could import his doctrine of monotheism and watch it work out to fulfilment; and he chose the Bedoni with their twelve leaders – a great people whom he could command through their leaders and they would obey.

These were the children of Israel, and at the time that Moses first approached them they had been taken prisoners, as it were, in a very subtle way by Rameses the Second, who, having enthralled them, decided to use them for the heavy rough work, for the hewing and the fashioning of the stones, for the great forts which he desired to build from Pelusium to Heliopolis, a vast tract of country which must be fortified against the invader. For Rameses was afraid. Great cities had grown on the banks of the Ganges and Euphrates, cities in which the kings ruled the priests, whereas in Egypt it was the priesthood that commanded the king; because the kings ruled the priests, the priests put matters before the kings as the kings wanted them – not as God wanted them, or as God directed them. Therefore, mighty and strong in the physical world, kings of Babylon and Nineveh grew and flourished – if one can call cities beset with vice and crime and greed and material power flourishing.

But they put fear into the heart of Rameses and, therefore, Rameses must build forts. He had not sufficient of his own people to build them, so he drew carefully these nomadic tribes towards the cities of Babylon and Nineveh and showed them the glories of the worship of Mammon and all the sin that beset the people of Babylon and Nineveh. From that he drew them, little by little, to slave in the great desert and haul and hew the stone and to prepare the forts, which should defend him later from the invader.

Moses knew he could not try out the doctrine of monotheism on just individual men here and there; he must have many, and so he approached the rulers of these people and he persuaded them to use the people; he became their leader; he showed them the glory of the world outside and the horror of slavery, and at the same time his messengers, who had the ear of Pharaoh, insisted that the Israelites be oppressed more and more, that Moses might appear more and more the deliverer, until the great day came when he was able to lead them away from Egypt, into the great wilderness where he taught them the things of God.

He found that the influence of Babylon had not abated, it was still strong in the older people, and in the young, because the older people had taught the young; therefore, from time to time he was called upon to administer justice with great severity, to prevent the worship of golden images and to insist that the people should turn to God. Because Moses was an initiate, the power of God worked through him, the very Being of God, and all that was necessary in the way of vision and the Voice of God and the miracle worked under the eyes of God, all these things were fulfilled before the eyes of the children of Israel, until in the end, they followed Moses their deliverer, Moses the initiate, who upon the mountainside received from the very 'Lips of God' the commands for the ruling of this people. These commandments are used today in your churches, and if a certain amount of the doctrine of hell fire and eternal punishment was mingled by the leader with the teaching which he gave them, it was essential, for they were a savage people, brought up in wild places, living wild lives, and only just recovering from the lash of the overseers and the brutality of the work of Rameses.

The Jewish people today are reincarnated Babylonians and have none of the simplicity of the Israelites of the past, but if you study the movements of the world in Israel and in other eastern countries and you watch the events of life, you will find that the whole of that Egyptian drama is being played out today, except that Moses, the initiate, is not with us in the flesh. We await a gentler leader in the approach of the Aquarian Christ; we are waiting and watching for leaders who will lead the people with the knowledge of the esoteric teaching of Egypt poured through them, by those who established that teaching in the inner chambers of the Sanctuary and the inner chamber of the heart.

We shall find growing up in our midst children who cannot be governed, or ruled under modern educational methods, and because of our knowledge we shall be gentle and understanding with them. We shall see that their first steps are guided with common sense, that they are not spoiled and indulged, for they have missions to fulfil and work to do. We shall remember that very close to Egypt, in the study of science, there was Chaldea, where the study of science was not so pure as in Egypt, for never has there existed a nation greater in knowledge of science than the Ancient Egyptians. They held it in the inner chamber behind the High Altar; only the priests had access to it, and now, in your world today, man has access to every incident of science. Is he going to turn his knowledge to use science with power for his own self-esteem, or is he going to see that his scientific knowledge builds up the knowledge of God and the way of God in the hearts of men?

You will come in touch more and more with scientific minds who are seeking God, who know that when they touch the door of the little chamber behind the High Altar they are not permitted to open it but who know that there are incarnate in the world, men and women of vision who have the key to that door. One day the scientist will have to go with humility to the mystic and the seer and say to them, 'I need your help for the end of my journey, open, I pray thee, the door of the Sanctuary that I may enter and study therein.'

The Chaldeans studied very much more astrology than astronomy; therefore, those who are incarnate today from Chaldea will turn their thoughts first to astronomy and then through astronomy will come to astrology. There are many things that we must know before we may touch the teaching within the little chamber behind the High Altar.

CHAPTER THIRTY

Egypt under Rameses II

At the period when Rameses II was upon the throne as Pharaoh, we see an immensely powerful, wealthy and dissolute court, and within that court we find a large number of brilliant men, scientists, architects, teachers and religious dignitaries; for the court and the temple in Egypt were as one, except that Pharaoh used the court; but in Atlantis the priests used the king; for the king and the priests in Atlantis were one – in Egypt the power of the Pharaoh was predominant.

Rameses was one of the greatest kings who ever ruled in Egypt. Cruel he was, that was his nature and his up-bringing, but at the same time it was the brilliance of his mind that was so outstanding, in all things at that day. He had a son, Meneptah; not a very prepossessing boy, delicate, caring very little for the sport and the outdoor exercise which was prescribed to all Egyptians of the Royal House, inclined to be indolent and withdrawn. He had tutors who were chosen for him and provided by the temple and it was the high priest of the Temple of Isis who commanded the young prince's studies.

From an early age Meneptah had a companion, a strange silent boy, brilliantly intelligent, quick to learn, quick to achieve; he could fulfil all the games that Meneptah shirked; he was a fine runner, strong in body, clear of vision, a fine swimmer; and all that he learned from the tutors, side by side with Meneptah, showed brilliance and wit and strength of purpose. He concealed his wit and all his life he was uncommunicative, treading dark silent ways alone in his free time, caring for none, seeking to do good to none, observant of all, and noting the most minute details in all that was said and done and thought.

This boy's name was Onesirus; he was also known as Osarsiph. He was the child who was found in the bullrushes by the Princess Royal of the court, and had been brought up side by side with Meneptah as a Royal Prince. He had only been a short while attached to the temple service when he was made a Levite, and because he was called a Levite he was reputed to be of the Jewish race; but Moses was never of Jewish blood, for this boy's name, which he took later, was indeed Moses. He showed no deep affection for anyone, only the desire to learn, and at every moment he escaped to the priests and scribes in the temple, that he might learn from them, not so much about sacred books and the rites of the temple as about men, and also about God.

There came a day when his mother drew him aside and reproached him for his silence and his desire to withdraw from the other princes at the court, and he told her then he had a mission in life. She reminded him that he was of the Blood Royal and could quite possibly be Pharaoh one day; but he explained he had no desire to sit upon a throne, all he desired was to learn to worship the one God. 'My son', said she, 'are not these Gods of Egypt great enough for thee that thou must seek a single Deity in the clouds' – 'Nay, Mother' he said, 'should I worship with a nation that speaks to God with the heads of animals and birds and beasts? – I seek for something of a very different nature from that.'

His work in the temple was of such satisfaction to the highpriest that he was given more and more responsibility which he fulfilled untiringly, building always in his own mind his service to God – never to Pharaoh or the court. It was the custom in Egypt that all princes sent to the temple for education should play their part on every occasion to which they were called, and it was not long before this man was given a very important position – to visit the nomes or divisions of the land of Egypt and through these visits to come in touch with the rulers and the people that inhabited them; to know what was right and what was wrong with the governance of these nomes; to form his own opinion and to bring back information to the temple.

Before he set out on his journeys he was called to the side of the Pontiff, the highest priesthood of the Temple of Isis, and he was called upon there by Membra to state his purpose in life, what he desired to do, which way he desired to follow, for it was important that the high priests of the temple should know the ideas in the head of this young man, who was to go forth on so important a mission.

Moses bowed the knee to no man; he made no obeisance to the Pontiff; standing tall and strong before him, placing his hands together in token of obedience, only. And Membra said, 'Where goest thou, my son? What dost thou want to do and to achieve in this great land of Egypt? Dost thou hunger for the throne? Dost thou desire to rule the country, or wilt thou withdraw into the silence, a place apart, to study religion and science and all that goes to the making of the land under the guidance of God? Wilt thou thus be an adviser to the Pharaoh?'

At the moment that this question was asked, Moses was standing beside the Ark of the Covenant of the Lord. The Ark with its beauty of gold leaf wrought in its carving and two angels with bowed heads and spread wings leaning forward over the precious receptacle which contained the wonderful teaching. Moses placed his hands together, and then one on the side of either angel, and he said to Membra. 'My Lord, I desire no power, nothing but the ability to worship God and to teach men to worship God and to learn through the symbolic writings of the past the way to God'. And ·Membra said, 'Within the Ark are the writings of the sacred Mysteries graven on stone in symbol – if thou desirest to read these thou must study many years in the temple, under those who know the meaning of the symbols'. Then Moses said, 'Nay, My Lord, not that do I desire either; these writings are dead, I can study the parchments of the scriptures and find more life in them than in the stones within the Ark of the Covenant. If the living spirit will communicate with me I prepare myself to listen – I need no dead voice to show me the symbols that pave the way to the knowledge of God.' 'Then, my son,' said Membra, 'What wouldst thou do when thou hast been given these teachings of the spirit', and Moses looked at him long – he said, 'I would divest myself of the robes of state, I would walk bareheaded and barefooted from one end of the court through the courtyards of the palace and back through the court again and there would I proclaim the God of Abraham, the God of Love, the One God of all men whose voice is truth.

'Dost thou then, my son,' said Membra 'find falsehood and untruth in the court, thou a mere boy desirest to bring forward words of a different nature from an unknown God for the Pharaoh to hear.' And Moses with humility pointed to the pathway to the temple up which strode a solitary figure wearing the robes of Pharaoh's son, his head bound with a scarf of the Levite, the feet sandalled on the smooth pathway of the temple. And he said, 'There, My Lord, thou seest him who has sought from childhood in the atmosphere of the court to touch the psychic and now seeks to open the door to the things of the occult world which God deplores' – and Membra bowed his head for he knew that the son of Pharaoh thought only about soothsayers and prophecies – and many of those were untrue and false, which he in his ignorance and his desire to hold to psychic matters would not deny.

Membra covered his head and returned to the temple. In the course of his journeys in the inspection of the nomes Moses found himself called upon to inspect the Delta, and here he found hundreds of thousands of men and women and children also, toiling in the service of Pharaoh, Rameses II. One family and their dependents were called to hew stone and make bricks, others prepared wood and metal, while others dragged about slabs of stone from great distances, and the hot sand of the desert scorched their feet and parched their mouths and the sun beat down upon their heads.

He moved among them telling them of God and His Love, telling them also something which we cannot accept today in all our religious beliefs – the bitterness of God against wrong doers and the punishments which were meted out for lack of truth and darkness. Moses told them of the things of the spirit

179

and of the voice of God, which spoke in the silence. Little by little, he called them together to the worship of God in the wilderness. There came a day when one of the finest youths who was leading these groups of worshippers was brutally ill-treated by an Egyptian overseer – and Moses ordered him to desist. The man continued and Moses slew him.

For this crime he had to leave the Delta and journey back to the Temple of Isis and there confess to Membra, before Membra the Pontiff, the high priest, his cruel misdeed. He was withdrawn from his visits to the nomes, but Membra realised that this was a spirit which could not be held in bondage, for that if there were to be any freedom for Moses' contemporaries, Moses must be educated in the knowledge of all things scientific, that he might rule the world of science and give the teaching to the children of men, and withdraw into the innermost sanctuary of the temple to listen for the voice of God, but let loose among the people of Egypt he could bring thoughts and desires of revolution to overthrow the Pharaoh and the court.

We know how Moses, after he had expiated his sorrow in the temple returned to the Delta; how he eventually led the toiling slaves of Pharaoh away from Egypt, how they crossed the Red Sea and hungered in the wilderness. During their bitterest suffering, Moses withdrew to the great mountain to hear the voice of God guiding his people. And they, perhaps, still believed that the Israelites were chosen by God as his chosen people – they were chosen, certainly, to fulfil a great work, a great mission, and to leave behind them a teaching which none but Moses could have given, or translated for their service. They were never intended to be the only men on earth whom God loved.

The Exodus is worth studying: Many of the events described in the Bible are wrong; there are mistakes, but the main story is there and the endurance and strength of spirit, the intelligence and determination of that great leader is one which no man who shared that experience can ever forget. The releasing of the Israelites from bondage is one of the great landmarks in the esoteric teaching which is being prepared to be given, not on tablets of stone, but by the voice of God, the living spirit speaking to your hearts as God spoke to Moses. There, in the Delta today are many stones with strange symbols upon them and many of these stones must be held in the mirror of the Nile and the waters splashed upon them, before they will reveal their secrets. They are carven symbols, carved under the guidance of Moses, which would give much truth and illumination in the story of the Red Sea. But every one of those miracles which God fulfilled with the Israelites have been and are being always fulfilled in the world of men. But men are blind. Those who have come from the world of spirit to give this teaching throughout many sanctuaries, and many small places where the children of God congregate, are here for one purpose only, to open your hearts that the living spirit of which Moses spoke can manifest through you.

For the light of the spirit dwells in the sanctuary and most deeply in the sanctuary of your own heart; but it can only dwell there if your heart is pure and true.

Be still and know that I am God, saith The Lord.

CHAPTER THIRTY ONE

Moses and the Israelites

After Moses had slain the Egyptian taskmaster he did not resist arrest. He was loaded with heavy chains and cast into prison to await the call of Pharaoh at his judgment seat. He took his physical punishment and condemnation as befitted a King's son, he murmured not, he used neither violence, nor strength, nor speech against his jailors; he stood with humility before the court and he heard the fatal words 'Let justice be done' from the lips of Pharaoh and the raising of the Flail.

The sentence was a heavy one, for the Egyptian whom he had slain was an important leader among those who prepared the architectural details for the great buildings which were in progress. He was taken in a chariot by jailors to a far distant desert, with his eyes blindfolded in such a way that he could not find the road back to Egypt. Egypt was no longer his home; he was condemned to eternal banishment.

In the desert without food or water he came very close to God in humility, and in prayer and supplication he accepted at the hand of God the working out of the moral, spiritual law, in the same way as he had accepted the physical punishment meted out to him on the earth. There were times when he was near death, but always the power of the spirit drew close to him in meditation, and in the acceptance of his desire to serve, until gradually a great light broke upon his mind and he realised that it was his task to band these oppressed people together and carry them out from the bondage of Pharaoh into the light of the one God, to proclaim the God of Israel – Jehovah.

It was strange that once he had arrived at this conclusion he no longer felt distress against the desert. The rays of the sun beating down upon him, the great heat which scorched his skin and parched his throat troubled him not; he walked with strength – in the body but in the spirit also, nourished entirely by the power of God – forward to his great mission.

When you read these stories in the Bible it sounds as if Moses returned to the Israelites practically at once and led them forth, but we must remember that they, too, had to complete their duty to Pharaoh – the expiation which had caused them to be held in bondage and broken by the yoke of Egypt.

There came a day when a gleam of green grass was visible on one of the crags of the great stones and rocks which lay in his path; he moved forwards towards it and fell down thanking God that he was near the end of his journey. It was night, and when the dawn came, flocks of sheep surrounded him, and he was held in conversation by three women who were tending the sheep for their father, Jethro. One ran quickly to Jethro and told him of the plight in which this traveller found himself, and Jethro came forth and gave him a staff and guided him to his tent. Then for many days, in great fever he lay and was delirious almost to madness from the suffering he had passed through.

Jethro was no ordinary man, he was a seer and an initiate, and, just as Moses' steps had been guided towards him, he knew, detail by detail, what he must do; he did not make Moses' path easy – there was still the spiritual expiation of his sin to fulfil but he did give him physical shelter and food and time to rest and restore himself.

We know that over and over again Moses went up alone into the mountains for long periods, and Jethro knew why, and who called him. And in those mountains the voice of God spake to him with strength and colour and delight; and he brought the messages back, but he told no man, he pondered them in his heart and planned his life towards their keeping.

He married Zipperah, one of the daughters of Jethro, and

dwelt in great happiness in that alien land, seeking no more the joys of Egypt, glad to be clear from the trammels of the court and the difficulties which he had faced. Now and again the sufferings of the oppressed people came into his mind and he would pace the ground by night and day in his endeavour to decide where his duty lay.

Jethro guided him towards great studies, and Moses covered many miles on foot, to the great temples, where, on the word of Jethro he was given an opportunity to read books and manuscripts which gave him the whole picture of the cosmology which he sought.

You will find part of that cosmology described in *Genesis*; but one of the most valuable manuscripts which Moses was permitted to read was burned in the great fire of the sacred volumes at Alexandria, a fire which was not accidental, which has lost us much of the great wisdom which could have opened the knowledge of the things of the spirit by modern man.

Gradually, Moses came to offer his service in the Temple of Isis. He came as a humble porter, he swept the floors, he brushed the hangings, he cleansed and prepared the altar vessels, and each time he entered the temple he knelt with humility before the altar and asked God for His blessing that he might be used as an instrument to build the true religion for the people of Israel, to prepare them as a fighting unit, to throw off the yoke of Pharaoh and go out clean and pure to accept at the hands of Moses, after his preparation, the teaching which was necessary to them as the builders of the race of Israel.

In his service in the temple, Moses learned many things; he learned that there were three distinct forms of teaching – a simple, clear teaching for the common man, for many of those who worshipped in the temples had no access to books, or writings, no learning of any description. They toiled in the fields and gathered the corn and threshed it, they planted the rice and listened to the waters of the Nile. The second form of teaching was symbolic and picturesque, given to those who attended the temple ritual and who were educated sufficiently to be able to understand the symbols. It was the symbol teaching, strengthened and exemplified, over the heads of the common people, but still not for the priests. The third form was sacred and hieroglyphic; therefore it could only be understood by the priests, trained to hold these symbols in their minds, to express them in hieroglyphs and to read both symbols and hieroglyphs when called upon to do so.

Moses greatly desired to understand the beginning of God's work, and he studied deeply for this purpose. He learned that the great cosmology of Egypt was there, for those who could read it. This cosmology is repeated in your *Book of Genesis*, but in a childish, rather foolish form, quite different from the way in which it was given in the temple. 'He learned that he must study the ancient Atlantean teachings that later were brought by Confucius, Buddha, and all the great Eastern teachers, the great faiths and writings of the past; and he learned also that he must study the synthesis of the preparation for initiation.'

For initiation must comprise the knowledge of the ancient religion and all that concerns the life of man, from God's first touch when he said 'Live, O man, and go forth in My name'.

We know the story of the Israelites, how Moses came disguised as a slave and was employed among the slaves, and how, little by little, he bound them together until they came to trust him. And having trusted him in the beginning, they chose him as a leader, and with fearless strength he went forward gathering together those who were ready and able to follow him, until eventually Pharaoh let them go and they departed from Egypt to the great wilderness. We must not forget that there was no one movement, one action, one thought of Moses undertaken without the guidance of God.

Although it may seem that his venture into Sinai concerned only the giving of the tablets of stone, he went many times to that great mountain where, covered in cloud from the gaze of anyone who should look and behold him, he spoke to God, face to face, and God directed his way. None of these things could have been fulfilled without the teaching of Jethro, not one of the incidents in Moses' life after his punishment in the desert could have been undertaken if he had not listened to that great seer and initiate and recognised him for what he was.

Now the whole cycle is back again; man toils under the yoke of man and calls for a deliverer. Which way will he come, from the north, or the south, from the east, from the west? And he cometh. And what will he do? His whole work is described by one word, synthesis.

One day all men will know the meaning of synthesis, for the New Christ who is the deliverer of mankind will possess all these qualities. He will bring with him, and open the door for all those who are ready, the whole history of the great religions of the past. He will show to those who are ready the hieroglyphs and the mysteries, the symbolic utterances of the guides and teachers and great beings who come to guide mankind, and He will open the door for all time, to those who are ready to accept at the hands of God, initiation into these mysteries.

But each must play his part, each must fulfil that contribution which he must make to that synthesis. When the time comes for you to be given the spiritual meaning of synthesis, the road will open and there will be no more doubt, no more wavering, no more hesitation. You will go straight forward even as Moses went from the temple to the camp of the Israelites, to lead them forth. They were not ready for the things of the spirit; he had to lead them through the wilderness, he had to see that they were left without food and sustenance that they might thank God for the heavenly food and drink; he had to prove to them step by step that the God of whom he spoke was a living Being guiding them, strengthening them, uplifting them. He had to watch them fall away and give way to orgies of a horrible nature; he chose from among them the right leaders; he learned to study the hearts of each one of them; they became a great people in the worship of the one true God.

We are going back on the cycle. Remember that part of the study in the temple always concerned involution, which means coming into physical life, and evolution which means going forth from physical life into a regenerated life beyond the normal vision of man. When you study involution and evolution you are making the complete circle. You have one foot on the ladder – the Ladder to God.

CHAPTER THIRTY TWO

The Death of Moses and the Coming of Orpheus

There were many peaceful years after the Israelites came out of bondage, but there were also years when darkness enfolded the people and they engaged in riots and dancing and unpleasant orgies which were distasteful to their leader. He found that it was no use endeavouring to stop these conditions; he therefore let them go through to the end and, when the people were completely darkened with the horror of what they had undertaken, he left them awhile to cleanse themselves before he called them to prayer.

It was at these moments that he called forth from among the Israelites men with knowledge of herbs and healing, who could prescribe cleansing potions and treatments for those who needed it. Some of these he applied to the whole people, others were applied individually. This was the first clinic ever founded, for it was those whom Moses called from among the people to prescribe for them, who came together at an appointed time to consult those who were learned in the power of the herbs, the cleansing of water and the treatment which today you call relaxation and therapy. It takes only a few moments to tell you of these matters, yet they go very much deeper and laid the foundation of great things in the future, which were later carried out by Greek and Roman doctors. The great business of medical treatment began in the desert.

Following these conditions, Moses, who was now a very old

man, found himself extremely fatigued; he looked over his people and saw that this was a period of labour; the time was used for improving the land, and the conditions of the people. He realised that there were growing up among them young men with intelligence beyond the average, and that they were preparing, first with sticks upon sand and then with lines made by the same sticks upon tablets of wet clay, plans which should be used in the building of harbours, houses and all the buildings which had been left behind in Egypt.

He felt that the time had come for him to withdraw. Calling to him Joshua and seventy of the Levites among the people, he departed towards Mount Sinai to dwell awhile in simplicity in the caves of the rock and in the silence of God. He left behind him a people working hard, singing with happiness, nurturing their families with strength and understanding, and he felt he could safely leave them and take his rest.

Night by night in the cave our Father-Mother God spoke to him, no longer of the things of the earth but of the things of the spirit. He told him that the bridge of death was very close to him, that though all men had feared that bridge before, Moses need have no fear, and God told him to call from among the Levites whom he had with him, a group of seven who would stand behind Joshua at the rising of the sun and at the going down of the sun, and thus hold the power of the Father-Mother God who wished to speak to Moses.

During these periods, Moses neither ate nor drank, he was entirely nourished by the power of the spirit, strengthened by the Light of God and enfolded in His Grace. Truth rested upon his lips and in his heart. He told God of his experiences upon the earth, and with groups of people and that one mighty group that rested beneath him in the Plain, of his fears for their future. And he told God also of individuals whom he would strengthen that they might eventually lead tribes, or groups of these stiff-necked people to a right conclusion.

With the past left behind, Moses was given a vision of the future. He saw the Children of Israel bathed in degradation, he saw them departing from the Law of God which he had given them, he saw the darkness above them and round them, aye, and within them, and he grieved sorely upon the

188

mountainside. Then he called Joshua to him and signified that he must return and tell the people what he had seen and heard that they might hold the picture in their hearts and guard themselves against it.

When he returned all was as he had left it; the fields were being cultivated, the harvest was being gathered, the land was being made more and more profitable for the use of man and the people were happy. And he said to Joshua, 'Lo, my vision is untrue; why has it led to me? why has it shown me this falling into evil ways and the darkness surrounding the people whom I taught about the one God, whom I have called to worship the one God, whom I have prepared as a people whom God could trust, whom He could use as His instruments in His Service in the way of Light.'

And Joshua said, 'Pardon me, O most noble leader, am I not right in believing that you are being withdrawn from the earth and that in that withdrawing you are being shown the future of the people, a very long way ahead?' Moses said, 'Shall I again withdraw into the silence of the mountain, that I may speak to God face to face and ask His will?'

This is the important point at this juncture in our story. Moses did not seek to build for himself, for his own vainglory, or advancement, any reward for what he had done with the Children of Israel, nor did he call upon God and say, 'See, I have brought this people out of evil ways and given them strength to serve Thee rightly.' He withdrew from them, that he might hear the Voice of God in the silence and speak to him face to face.

This time he took with him only Joshua and two of the lesser Levites to serve them, and they climbed the mountain of Sinai higher than before and found within the side of the mountain a greater cave than the one in which Moses had dwelled last time. Here they guided the old, old man, his sight failing, his body almost unable to surmount the roughness of the way, and they placed a large, flat stone for him in the entrance to the cave that he might watch the rising of the sun and meet God, face to face. At the bidding of Moses, Joshua and the two lesser Levites withdrew to a part where they could not see him, or hear him, although in their hearts they feared

189

something might happen to him and they would not be there to succour him.

Death came slowly to the aging man. His eyes dimmed more and more, his limbs became rigid so that he could not move and yet there was always the Glory of God with him and around him to bring him peace. The moment of death came at the moment of the rising sun. And there stood in the entrance of the cave an angel holding in his left hand a ball of flame and in his right hand the sword which severs the chains of earth from a man of God.

And Moses saw, he saw that he could see, not with the physical eye but with the eye of the spirit, for he took the angel by the hand and he led the angel himself, and they left the cave behind and they mounted through the ether from the grey fur of the earth into the lighter, stronger and more exquisite ethers of the heights, until there felt no more weight, no more horror, no more sorrowing for the children of the earth, only a great and glorious joy surrounded with praise and thankfulness to God that he could have brought him so great a reward.

The light of the angel dimmed as the angel withdrew. For a moment Moses felt his soul to be alone, but he faltered not; he went forward and the Light of God surrounded him and held him, and the Light of God was greater than the light of the angel of death, and the angel of death had brought him to God at a moment when his work was finished and completed and the glory of his soul was given in service to God, for God to do with him as He willed. Moses knew no fear. He spoke to God of the visions in the cave, of the horror that his people could defile the earth and could retreat so far from the teaching he had given them to break the great tables of the law and forget the God of their Fathers.

A scribe explained to him, 'My son, you are being given the vision of the future; you will see your people drag the world into the mire and the horror of carnage and war, battle and sudden death, and you will return to guide the deliverer of the world whom you are now called upon to meet. And behind the Voice of God – for no figure of God appeared – behind the Voice of God their stretched a great radiance, drawn out from

190

the centre where the voice came, and a great light illumined and enlarged the whole of the heavens. And within that light there came a lesser radiance, and one appeared as a pilgrim in a brown habit and a hood over the head, his sandalled feet were bare, he had a beard, he showed in his bearing great gentleness and yet the knowledge of the work which he would one day do upon the earth was pouring from his eyes, so that Moses read his life as he realised the greatness he was meeting. He bowed his head and fell upon his knees and placed his face upon the ground, for he had met the Lord Jesus who would in due time come to earth, to deliver those very people Moses had also delivered. But Moses delivered them from the bondage of man in the material world, this Christed One would deliver them from the bondage of the soul; He would teach men to see God through their own hearts, for Moses had met Jesus Christ.

While all these things were happening, while Moses was withdrawn more and more from contact with the Children of Israel, a new age, and a new faith and a new light was being born in Greece. For in Greece their appeared a young man of exceptional beauty, a young man whom artists and sculptors would want to mirror in clay and in stone and in colour, down through the ages, with a body of such perfection and physical grace no man since has ever copied it – for this was Apollo.

Apollo was weary of the following the people gave him wherever he went, and he departed to a far country and dwelled for a long time with the Hyperboreans, and there, there was born to him a son whom the Gods desired him not to name until he was told by the invisible voice, the name. The son was brought in a vessel down a great water into Greece, and the son was in the charge of a high priestess who commanded the swans that led the boat into its rightful place. The journey took a long time; though the child was an infant when he embarked, he was a boy of twelve when the boat touched the shores. And the high priestess guarded and guided him and directed his steps towards a temple which had taken twelve years to build and prepare for him and had been prepared at the command of his father.

Apollo was renowned throughout Greece wherever he had

191

been for the glory of his voice, but even more the singing voice which was a perfect pitch, a natural pure Godlike note. But the son had no voice at all to speak of until he had covered the age of twentyone years and then the high priestess who had brought him to the Grecian shore presented him with a golden key, and as he opened the door of the inner sanctuary of the temple his voice came. But even as a small boy he was greatly skilled with the instruments of metal, and the triangle sounded notes through the temple that none had ever heard before; gradually the notes of the triangle were captured by another instrument and the first stringed instrument was produced and used in the temple service.

This boy was comely also, but not in the same way as his father, for his father had the physical beauty of the earth and the glory of the world of sound in his voice. But this boy had the power to produce sound from the invisible ethers by simply remaining stationary in the centre of the temple. The most amazing notes of music, the glory of the spheres come down to man, because he could produce this by merely sitting still; all men could hear it who were ready and learned in the temple service. For the triangle played when no-one touched it and the notes of the lyre trilled through the temple when no hand was upon it, and the voices of angels and teachers and great heavenly choirs surrounded the boy in the temple till he knew not where he was.

The Father-Mother God commanded that the boy should be trained in the temple service and should begin from the bottom and learn the humble duties of the postulant, that he should reach out through that humble work in service to the Glory of God. He was sent away to Egypt and here, under the highpriest of Memphis, treated as one of the ordinary farmer's sons, dedicated to the temple service, he was trained from every angle of the temple work, in all the simplicity of the lessons and the service until he was ready to return to Greece, with the knowledge of the purpose of his life, of the power of the invisible worlds and how he could use the power of these worlds for good in service to God. When he left the temple the highpriest placed upon each shoulder a symbol of a golden wing, and called him Orpheus.